SHOWGIRL CONFIDENTIAL

PLEASANT GEHMAN

Punk ♛ *Hostage* ♛ *Press*

Showgirl Confidential
Pleasant Gehman

ISBN 978-1-940213-75-0
© Punk Hostage Press 2013

Punk Hostage Press
P.O. Box 1869
Hollywood CA, 90078
www.punkhostagepress.com

Introduction
Iris Berry

Foreward
Steve Balderson

Cover Design
Natasha Vetlugin

Cover Photo
Dusti Cunningham

INTRODUCTION

It was the summer of 1983 when Pleasant Gehman and I started our long and illustrious friendship. The first time we really bonded was literally in a gutter, over a cheap bottle of wine. There we were, sitting on a curb in Hollywood, on the corner of Hudson Avenue and Santa Monica Boulevard, as I'm trying to muster up the courage to go into this particular club and do an open-mic reading of my poetry, and Pleasant was lamenting over her current relationship, which was falling to pieces. Needless to say, we never made it inside the club, and besides, what was going on in that gutter was far more important.

Three days later, at about four in the morning, I dreamt that Pleasant was banging on my bedroom window, urging me to wake up because she was cruising around Hollywood in a purple metal-flake hearse, with a full bar and a German guy (whom she'd just met) named Filthy McNasty, and a couple of his friends, who just happened to be dwarves. I declined her generous offer and settled into the next dream, (nothing as exciting as a hearse full of dwarves and hard liquor, I assure you). The next day I called Pleasant to tell her about my crazy dream of how she was banging on my window inviting me to come on a hearse ride. She informed me that it wasn't a dream and that it did happen, and how I really missed out, and to this day, Pleasant, I want you to know, I still regret not getting out of bed.

When Pleasant and I were in our early 20's, living together at our place, Disgraceland, she was starting her band, The Screaming Sirens, she told me the fact that she was able to master Ms. Pac-Man was proof to her that she could successfully start a band and go on tour. I laughed, but she was right.

For Pleasant Gehman, nothing is impossible. Everything she puts her hands on, she creates beauty and inspiration. She is proof that we *can* get better and more beautiful with age. She is more stunning now than ever. And my life would not be the same without her. More than an introduction, this is a love letter, with great honor, respect, deep love and affection. Pleasant Gehman, my sister, my wife, my glamorous guardian angel through some of the wildest years in the punk rock Hollywood underground, and the love of my life. I have never met anyone like her. The best way I can say it is, Pleasant Gehman is *Other Worldly*.

Pleasant lives like she writes and writes like she lives. She's the real deal. She's obsessed, possessed and driven. I imagine that if I didn't know Pleasant Gehman and found her books. It would be a monumental occasion like it has been the times I've discovered all of my favorite writers, where I would read her over and over to everyone I knew that hadn't heard of her yet.

I suppose in essence that's what I'm doing now. I'm urging you. I'm urging you to take that ride in the purple metal-flake hearse, and every other wild ride with Pleasant Gehman, that is between these pages. It will definitely change your life.

-Iris Berry

FOREWORD

I first met Pleasant Gehman when I attended a reading she was giving at Skylight books in Los Angeles. I heard her voice before I laid eyes on her. She was laughing wildly, greeting fans and countless admirers. When I saw her, she took my breath away. I'd never seen a movie star or a princess up close before. She was dazzling in a turquoise dress with rhinestones, glitter and feathers exploding from her wavy dark hair. I'm pretty sure she was wearing a tiara.

I walked over to her and introduced myself. When she looked at me, I felt her eyes going right through my soul. It was weird, but it was like time stopped, and I had a suspicious feeling we already knew each other. From a past life, or something equally supernatural. It was electric. And what was super cool... I could tell she felt the same thing. We didn't get much time to visit at the reading but it was comforting to know we had an innate special connection.

The first real time we had the opportunity to bond, it was at the Cannes Film Festival in the south of France. My first film was screening at the festival and Pleasant had a song on the soundtrack.

Plez arrived on the Riviera a day or so after I did. She was coming from Paris and although suffering a broken heart, we carried on like a house on fire, laughing uncontrollably and having the time of our lives. We flirted with the same wine steward, held court in the lobby bar at the Carlton, and played games like, "Is That Celebrity Insane?" People like Michael Stipe came up to Plez and said things like, "You're my favorite writer!"

I was constantly amazed by the incredible life force and positive energy surrounding her at all times. After watching Pleasant belly dance down the middle of the Croisette with my brother who was dressed as a giant condom, I realized what anybody who knows Pleasant already knew: her stories are legendary and endless. And this book will prove it.

Over the years our friendship and bond has strengthened. On a totally personal and magic level, Pleasant Gehman saved my creative life.

I was at a crossroads in my early film career, and struggling to find inspiration. I learned that Pleasant would be teaching a belly dance workshop in Nebraska, so I decided to go film it for her. I knew Plez performed belly dance under the name Princess Farhana, and I knew she made instructional belly dance videos. I thought it could be something she might be able to use as a bonus feature.

The workshop was full of mostly women, all different shapes and colors and sizes. On stage in front of the class, Plez pushed her belly out and grabbed it with both hands, claiming it. Instructing everyone in the room to go against what society tells you, and instead, to embrace who you are, and to appreciate your own natural body. When I saw her doing that, a fire lit inside me. I knew I had to document this woman. What she was teaching was revolutionary. I knew the whole world needed to see this and to learn from her. I followed Her Royal Highness and captured a year in her life for what would become the feature documentary *Underbelly*. In addition to becoming a world-renowned belly dancer, Pleasant was also a fantastic burlesque dancer. Combining elements of the two would make Princess Farhana one of the most controversial performers in that world. And like any true pioneer, she paved the way for an entirely new generation of dancers and performers.

Pleasant Gehman is a true renaissance woman. She's an amazing poet, writer, dancer, actress, composer, painter, businesswoman, and a marvelous chef. And her friendship is a treasure. She is an inspiration and she's helped inspire many, many people. If you have the opportunity to meet her, or take a class from her, or travel with her, or laugh with her, you should grab the chance and do it. There is no one in the world like Pleasant.

She's a glittering tornado, a Tasmanian Rhinestone. And if you're as lucky and as honored as I have been, you will likely end up part of her wild adventure.

-Steve Balderson

"You only live once…but if you do it right, once is enough."

-Mae West

Thank you and lots of Breathy Hollywood
Air Kisses to the following people, who all took part in some of
these adventures: James Packard, DeVilla, Maharet Hughes,
Steve Balderson, my Flying Monkeys Natasha & Kelly,
Jane Wiedlin, Margaret Cho , Bobby McCLellan,
and of course to my family.

* * *

This book is dedicated to my lifelong friend,
partner in crime, twin soul and now, publisher, Iris Berry.
Here's to our future, racing up and down the halls of The Punk
Rock Showgirl Rest Home in our tricked out, rhinestone-
bedazzled wheelchairs. I love you babe...
it *is* babe, isn't it?

TRUE SMUT

I was an extremely precocious child. From the time I was just out of diapers, it seemed I was always hyper-aware of sensuality. I was fascinated by the power of seduction at an age where I not only couldn't pronounce the word, I had no idea what it meant or that such a thing even existed. But I could *feel* it, and knew somehow that those nameless things I was feeling were very important.

Some of my earliest childhood memories involve flirtation and longing. When I was three, I was infatuated with my half-brother Scott, eight years my senior. He told me what the word "crush" meant, and I took it literally, feeling like a cartoon safe had been dropped on my head every time I stole a lingering glance at him.

However, I was already a seasoned *player*. In a paean to Beatnik Chic, I wore black cat-eye sunglasses with stretch pants and a beret as an every day outfit, looking like a miniature version of an Italian movie star. I even owned a slinky leopard maillot. I fell in and out of love with an alarming regularity. Had I been, oh, a decade and a half older, I definitely would have been called a tramp.

So it was at that tender age that my whole family was traveling from New York to Los Angeles. My father, well-known entertainment writer who had recently completed a book called *Sinatra And His Rat Pack,* was off to "The Coast" for a series of interviews that would turn into *That Kid*, his biography of comedian Jerry Lewis. Because he'd be in LA for months, he'd brought our entire brood along for some fun in the sun.

The plane was crowded, and one of the passengers was Henry Morgan, a well-known television talk show host, famous for his cantankerous contempt of children. Even though he knew exactly who my father was, before the aircraft even took off, Morgan was complaining loudly to the stewardess about my year-old brother Charlie's loud, teething-induced crying.

Oblivious of the man's disgust at being seated near a crying brat, I adjusted my beret to a jaunty angle and casually sauntered down the aisle to his row, where he sat with a mink-swathed glamorous blonde. Leaning my elbows on the arm of his chair, I stared deeply and soulfully into his eyes for at least forty-five seconds, then sighed dreamily, "You're *handsome!*"

Not only did Mr. Morgan become thoroughly charmed by my flagrant display, his Gabor Sister look-alike companion was beside herself, letting me try on her pearls and pet her fur stole. Even though Charlie didn't stop squalling once, the rest of the voyage a piece of cake. It turned out that Mr. Morgan talked about me incessantly on the air for a better part of a week, lauding me as the most charming and well-behaved child the man had ever met. Finally, I was invited onto the show as an on-the-air guest. Flattery, as they say, will get you *everywhere*.

No man was safe.

I had simultaneous crushes on our milkman, a gawky Buddy Holly type in a blinding white, bow-tied uniform, and also on our garbage man Mr. Mead, whom I remember as being a filthy gargantuan, ruddy with sunburn. A tattered, sun-bleached T-shirt stretched across his ample belly, he was never without a grimy pair of work-gloves and a dirty, battered baseball cap, smiling jovially and singing as he tossed around our battered aluminum trashcans. He called my mother "Missus", and I literally wanted to *be* him when I grew up. Mr. Mead was the sole reason I wanted a dump truck- so badly I could feel it in every fiber of my being- for Christmas the year I turned five.

At the same time, I was also in love with Peter Noone of Herman's Hermits, and a Manhattan traffic helicopter pilot named Fred Feldman. Basically I was into seeing his helicopter swirling above the George Washington Bridge as we drove into New York City, while simultaneously hearing his voice on the car radio. After I sent him a crayon drawing and he reciprocated with a signed 8 X 10 glossy of himself, dashing in a flight suit and grinning like a movie star, I decided I was going to *marry* him... although that didn't stop me from getting the shivers over Richard Burton, whose recitation of Hamlet I insisted on listening to -alternating with "The Story of Little Toot, The Tug Boat"-as a bedtime story.

I seriously lusted after my kindergarten classmates, and would've gladly died for the teenage Disney cowboys Spin and Marty. Unaware that amorous feelings were supposed to be directed only towards humans, I was obsessed with Astro Boy for his valor, Topo Gigio for his naughtiness, and Mr. Ed for his dry, sarcastic sense of humor. Monsters fascinated me, and I fed my habit by begging my mother to buy me horror movie magazines instead of dolls. I lost it over misunderstood, underdog mutants like Frankenstein's Monster, The Creature From The Black Lagoon, The Phantom of The Opera and Godzilla, whose

14

radioactive flame-spitting and rampant destruction of Tokyo turned me on to no end. Of course, like the rest of the country, I was also obsessed with The Beatles.

Having run through every possible infatuation, I then decided prudently to marry someone I knew inside and out: my baby brother Charlie. We were quite serious about our betrothal until we were made to understand that siblings couldn't be joined in holy matrimony. Ever practical, we made a joint announcement to the family that we simply wouldn't tell anyone that we were brother and sister. But with my fickle nature, even *that* passed.

My philandering eye was constantly roving, and soon I made friends with the all neighborhood kids, playing Kickball and Running Bases in the street. But after a couple of weeks of my influence, those white bread games had degenerated into far more *interesting* pastimes like playing doctor. We'd all be at Kathy King's playhouse, ostensibly to read her vast collection of Archie comics. Always the instigator, I was *never* the doctor, always preferring the infinitely hotter role of patient. I'd suggest some form of "operation", then strip off my Carter's undies and hop up onto the kid-sized tea-table, eyes shut in anticipation, waiting to get poked and prodded in a deliciously dirty way, by whomever dared.

When playing doctor became passé, I gave up vanilla sex for S&M. At my decree, we played "Concentration Camp"- and I was *always* the evil warden, barking orders and torturing the inmates. It was then I discovered my true switch-hitting nature, able to flit effortlessly between beings, as they say in The Lifestyle, a top or a bottom. Concentration Camp was a simply *wonderful* way to while away the endless summer afternoons, tying up my playmates, flogging them with sticks, screaming that they were pigs and force-feeding them cups of Tang! Powdered Orange Drink Mix combined with grass cuttings, dirt, Wishbone Thousand Island dressing, Comet Cleanser and 7-Up.

But then Charlie came up with something far better.

Our mother was employed at Wesleyan University, a men's college in Middletown, Connecticut. We lived on a broad, hilly street lined with Victorian mini-mansions, most of which had been converted in fraternity houses. It seemed Charlie (shades of Mr. Mead!) had discovered untold treasures in the frat house garbage cans, while delivering *The Middletown Press* on his paper route.

"Follow me," he whispered, out of the side of his mouth like a gangster.

He shrugged off his taxi-yellow canvas newspaper carrier, and wheeled his bike into the garage.

"You gotta see this!"

Curiosity piqued, I waited impatiently for him to show me what was so special. Sometimes, with great sincerity, Charlie would relate stories about incidents that were supposed to have occurred on his paper route… things that seemed so crazy they *had* to be true. He told me that one customer, a lady in her seventies, began chanting rhythmically, over and over, the second he pressed the buzzer:

"SOMEONE RANG THE DOORBELL, SOMEONE RANG THE DOORBELL!"

He said he could hear her in the house getting louder the closer she got to open the front door. Apparently, she'd actually danced onto the porch *nude*, still chanting at the top of her lungs as she dug into her change purse to pay him. I had no doubt this really happened; it wasn't until we were well into our twenties that he confessed to making that-as well as other tall tales- up.

Charlie took his time putting his carrier sack and bicycle away, and just when I was about to explode with anticipation, he pulled out an edition of *The Middletown Press*. He opened it slowly and with great care, revealing what was hidden inside: a dog-eared paperback book, whose plain olive green cover had printed boldly upon it: *69 Sex Street*.

I gasped in awe while he held it carefully, showing it off. Though we were unsure of the significance of the number 69, it did say "sex"-*that* we understood! Though neither of us could imagine why one of the main characters, a "busty redhead" named Carole, would allow a "well endowed" guy named Joe to stick a candle up her "yearning asshole", we were hooked…and we also knew that this discovery definitely had to be kept under wraps. Every day after school, we'd rush to the garage and take turns marveling over it, pulling it out of each other's hands.

The next week, Charlie brought home more spoils: three copies of *Playboy*, two of *Penthouse*. We spent all our free time before dinner skipping our favorite after-school TV program, *Dark Shadows*, paging through the magazines in stunned amazement, poring over the joke columns, the "swinging" cocktail recipes and "The Playboy Advisor" column.

16

Charlie was enthralled with the women- who were sprawled out on beds, couches and on rugs in front of roaring fires. There were naked women lounging on motorcycles, diving into swimming pools and sunbathing on the beach. Totally bare-assed "Bohemian" girls in berets, brushes and palette in hand, posing next to paint-splattered canvases. Girls clinging to yacht sails or spread-eagled on the hoods of sports cars; there were prairie scenes with "squaws" wearing stylized Indian war paint and feathers in their hair riding on horseback. Voluptuous vixens with huge bouffant hairdo's, opera-length gloves, and stiletto heels, coyly unzipped evening gowns. Naked hippie foxes wearing nothing but love beads, stood in fields holding big bouquets of wild flowers. Nude black women with bushy Afros reclined luxuriously under black light posters. Swedish blondes with caterpillar-like false eyelashes ate bon-bons while soaking in a bubble bath. There were Mod chicks clad only purple lace-up go-go boots and Twiggy make-up.

Turning more pages, I saw halfway-naked women becoming *more* naked, their grins naughty and inviting as they peeled off tennis outfits or the top half of men's pajamas. Snow bunnies topless under parkas, pursing their lips over steaming mugs of cocoa and wild-haired women holding wrenches, their faces smeared with motor oil, wearing mechanic's overalls unzipped to the crotch. There was a shopper with full grocery bags who was prettily surprised that her panties were around her ankles and a girl standing on a wharf, lifting up a rustic, cable-knit man-sized fisherman sweater, exposing rock hard nipples and countless photos of carefree gals frolicking with surfboards, showing off spectacular tan-lines.

Charlie found more magazines- *Rogue, True Detective, Cavalier, Stare, Gent,* and more copies of *Playboy* and *Penthouse,* until there was a huge stack, which he smuggled up to his room in the attic. He'd retire each night after dinner, ostensibly to do homework, but I knew better.

One night I knocked on his door and when there was no answer, pushed the door ajar. He was lying on his bed, propped up by see-through vinyl blow-up pillows emblazoned with traffic signs. He was lounging like a suave big-business magnate in his blue terry cloth bathrobe, reading a Playboy. This wasn't really anything new, he'd always had aspirations to executive glamour, his idols being first Howard Hughes and more recently, Hugh Hefner, but I was shocked to see that he was smoking a Tiparillo cigar, as advertised in Playboy.

"Come in, *come in,*" he said expansively, like a grown-up, gesturing with his cigar, getting up to lock the door behind me.

That night, he showed me his favorite centerfold, carefully bookmarked. There was Miss December, the "buxom, lovely" Cynthia Meyers, fetching and full of Christmas cheer in nothing but a Santa hat.

"Look at her tits," Charlie said, enthusiastically, as he tapped his Tiparillo, which had no doubt also been salvaged from a frat house trash can,

"They look just like *ski-slopes*!"

Though I liked seeing all the naked women, I hadn't been nearly as absorbed as Charlie with the pictorials of, as he called them, "nude girls". I was more obsessed with real-life girls, like the neighborhood prisoners I tied up and terrorized, or the Italian teenagers whirling around in skimpy skirts at the Holiday Roller Skating Rink. Even the older broads with frosted hair who hung around the shoe rental counter at Gilletti's Bowl-o-Drome fascinated me. I usually preferred 69 *Sex Street* or the letters section in *Penthouse* to the photo-spreads, because I could use my imagination, but that night everything seemed somehow... *different*.

Charlie had a point, the nude girls were indeed great. I suddenly had the uncanny revelation that it wasn't just the intricate skating moves or pierced ears and shag-hairdo that I was into. I'd always been excited by older men, and had seen them as sex objects, but now I was also fascinated by females. I realized that I'd been taking them for granted because, I, too, was female. I have to credit my baby brother for turning me on to women at the tender age of ten and a half.

Simultaneously, as I was becoming acquainted with my own sexuality, Charlie and I both realized we'd been sitting on a gold mine. *If we were this interested in these magazines, other kids would be, too!* Since nobody else had access to the magazines, we figured we could *sell* them. The problem was, they were so big, there'd be no way we could fit them into our lunch boxes and sneak them onto the playground at school. We came up with a plan. We'd make our own magazine! It was perfect- between Charlie's entrepreneurial skills and my abilities in writing and illustrating, we could do everything ourselves, from production to sales. All we had to do was decide on a name and a price.We'd split the profits down the middle.

True Smut was born that night, as was our career as pornographers. The formula was simple: as "the creative one", I was given artistic license as to the content, though we'd both come up with headlines and story titles. Charlie already had provided all the magazines, and it was his job to cut

18

out whichever photos I deemed useful and paste them into place. We decided on a pocket-sized format, so we could go for volume sales at maximum secrecy. We stole my mother's stapler, a bottle of Elmer's Glue, some magic markers, and got started.

Production took almost a week. We worked feverishly when Charlie got home from his paper route, and again after dinner. Sometimes, we'd even sneak out of bed and work from Charlie's closet. Every aspect, from quality control to editorial content as well as the fake Letters To The Editor detailing extraordinary sexual experiences, was overseen with painstaking attention to detail. We came up with vast numbers of titillating scenarios- with inspiration drawn from *69 Sex Street*, as well as our own prurient -but hideously naïve and misinformed- imagination. I remember there was even an illustrated scenario done in Bic Ballpoint Pen involving a woman who tried to make her sagging breasts perkier by rolling them around old-fashioned hair-curlers.

When we finally finished, our first run was ten issues. That may seem small, even for a limited edition, but it was a massive undertaking when you realize that I had to *hand write every single one of them...* Xerox or even mimeograph, due to our limited venture capital, not being an option. Then there was the problem of photo continuity. Since we only had one issue each of our source magazines, we were forced to use different photos for the same story in each copy of the book. We lucked out with the cover, though. Every magazine had the same one, thanks to a discarded pile of Wesleyan Theater programs we'd heisted from my mother's office. It had a comic book-style drawing of a naked girl standing under a spotlight, which was perfect for *True Smut*. All we had to do was cut it out, add our logo and price- we'd settled on a quarter- and we were good to go.

Covers in place, we were ready to sell our stock. That morning before school, we each took five. I gloated over my own handiwork- all the finger-cramps and blisters had been worth it, the final product looked dynamite! Our classmate's eyes practically popped out of their heads when they saw what we were hawking on the playground, and by the end of recess, we'd sold out the entire first edition of *True Smut*.

By lunch, we were busted. Some careless fourth grader had let one of the magazines fall out of his notebook in full view of the teacher. He was interrogated by the principal, and under extreme duress, ratted us out.

Unfortunately, our mother was notified. Fortunately, even though she acted appropriately appalled in front of the principal, she actually thought the whole incident was funny, and we weren't punished. We never had to return the money we made, either.

Though my short-lived career as a pornographer was over, and the neighborhood kids no longer fell for my sadistic scenarios, it was only a matter of time – barely a year and a half- until I turned into a teenager.

It was then, I was sure, that the *real* fun would begin.

GET YOUR KICKS ON ROUTE 666

My sister, my daughter...my daughter, my sister...She's my sister- and my daughter!

I was standing on my kitchen steps in a t-shirt and panties at 6:00 am, punctuating my hysterical Dramatic Recitation by slapping myself across the face. I had absolutely *no idea* why I felt the need to be play-acting the most infamous scene from Roman Polanski's 1974 neo-noir hit "Chinatown". For some unknown reason, I'd woken up with this frenzy-in minute detail- running through my head. It was almost as though I was being manipulated by some unseen force.

My new boyfriend Pa regarded me affectionately-and a little curiously-as he handed me a cup of coffee.

"What are you doing?" he asked affably, as though this wasn't such an unusual display at the crack of dawn.

I explained that I was acting out both the Faye Dunaway and Jack Nicholson parts from the scene where Evelyn Mulray, under duress from sadistic private dick Jake Gittes, breaks down and admits to the incest in her family.

"Oh," he said, nodding as though this was a perfectly logical answer,

"I never saw *Chinatown*, but I heard it was good!"

There was a reason Pa wasn't fazed by my behavior. Even though we were in the throes of new love, we'd actually known each other for ages and had a lot of history together. We'd met in the 1990's at the now-legendary Clown Party, an epic private event held at the Phoenix Iron Works warehouse in Oakland, California. Hundreds of people from every facet of the Bay Area's Alternative Scene attended: punks, visual and performance artists, skateboarders, college students and mad scientists from Survival Research Labs - all dressed like clowns. Pretty much the whole party was tripping their brains out on massive amounts of the freshly picked psilocybin mushrooms that the host, Steve Heck, had thoughtfully left out as party favors.

Like any rational, well-adjusted person, I *detested* clowns. But one glance at Pa, handsome in his painstakingly applied whiteface and a professional-looking red nose changed that. He was the sexiest clown I had ever seen. The following day, sans make up, he was even sexier. He had a dangerous, brooding Bad Boy appeal and a beautiful smile. I was beyond smitten…also, I had a *husband*.

Pa's real name was James. "Pa" was an old Army moniker, an abbreviation that had come from the first two letters of his last name, Packard. He'd been stationed in various Asian jungles for two years, and after being discharged he'd come to San Francisco to attend art school. It was a hot combination- he was a robust, ripped alpha male who could carry on conversations about classical literature and art theory. Though he'd grown his crew-cut out into a long, braided rat-tail that fell to his hips, some of his Army habits died hard; he was never without combat boots and still wore a bandanna tied around his head pirate-style, something he'd picked up in Thailand to prevent leaches from crawling into his ears while he slept on the ground. He told me insane Army stories- stuff like getting fully suited up in HAZMAT gear and gas masks during all-night chemical drills and taking two or three hits of acid to stay awake.

Whenever I'd come up to the Bay Area, he'd make special trips from his little ranch in Healdsberg to see me, but nothing ever happened, so I couldn't tell if he felt the same way about me. We'd get shit-faced at Oakland dive bars like Esther's Orbit Room, but all we ever did was hold hands. Besides, even after I'd broken up with my husband, both of us had always been with other people…then he married suddenly and disappeared, I was left heartbroken. More than a decade later I still thought of him constantly, so I worked my romantic demons out by writing a story about him called "Coco The Zombie Clown From Heaven, which was published in my memoir, *Escape From Houdini Mountain*.

In early 2002, years after his wife died and long after he'd broken up with the girlfriend who followed her, Pa was living in New Mexico. Someone had given him my book as a gift, asking if the story was about him. He read it and found me immediately, less than four months before the "Chinatown" moment unfolded. For once, our timing was *perfect*- he was single and I was just beginning to get over a cougar-iffic love affair with a Euro-trash artist who was fifteen years my junior. I was excited, but also extremely gun-shy. James had meant so much to me for so long, that the first time he came out to visit me, I decided I wasn't going to sleep with him. No matter what happened, it would undoubtedly end badly; if it were awful, it would ruin our friendship. But if it were great, I would be more in love than I already was…and because he lived in a different state that would suck.

I held out for exactly seventeen hours.

Naturally, we slept together and of course it was amazing. The next morning, I was appearing as the principle dancer in a video for a hip-hop artist called Truth Hurts. Her song "Addictive" had Arabic and Indian samples in it, and I'd been hired to belly dance in the club scene. Because it was my birthday, I made the executive decision to bring Pa to the set with me- I'd never brought a guest to a shoot before. When we arrived at the location, we were shocked to see stars like Snoop Dog, Dr. Dre, Eric B and Rakim, all of whom were making cameo appearances. The set was so thick with reefer smoke it was like a 'hood version of a Cheech And Chong movie, only it was *real*. The make up artist had to come around every five minutes to drop Visine into the guest star's bloodshot eyes, it was that bad. After the shoot, we were as inseparable as was humanly possible, given our long-distance romance.

The reason Pa and I were awake so early that "Chinatown" morning was because we were about to embark on a road trip back to his place in Santa Fe. Pa loaded up his new ride- a dilapidated 1970's pick-up truck, riddled with rust, its hideous yellow ochre paint sun-bleached and dotted with liberal amounts of Bondo and primer. The truck's deck had a makeshift bed, a rotten piece of foam covered by old moving blankets, and was crowned with an ugly, rotting brick-red camper shell, awash with Fiberglass splinters. People were always giving him vehicles that were destined for the junkyard, and he'd drive them into the ground with screw drivers stuck into the ignition, their engines literally held together with plastic twist-ties from garbage bags. After making a picnic of sandwiches, I threw my computer and a baby blue duffle bag full of cosmetics, high heels and slutty undies into the backseat, and we took off heading east on Interstate 10.

The truck hiccupped and creaked along as we laughed uproariously, discussing everything from our childhoods to what had happened to mutual friends from Phoenix Iron Works. With a dog-eared map spread on my lap, I recited the odd names of the tiny desert towns we'd pass through. In no hurry at all, we planned to drive til we couldn't anymore and stay overnight at some shitty motel- it didn't matter where- we'd just carry on with the 1,366-mile journey at our own pace. We stopped a couple of times for Slurpees and ice cream, browsing leisurely for souvenirs at truck stops, and wandering around rest areas in the arid heat, inspecting the vintage adobe Visitor Centers, marveling at massive cacti and eavesdropping on the other motorists gathered around the wind-worn picnic tables.

The periwinkle desert twilight had long turned to cool darkness by the time we pulled into Kingman, Arizona, 318 miles east of Hollywood. As Pa fueled up the truck, I admired the Atomic Age motel next to the service station, before noticing that the total of the gas purchased was $9.11. Though usually pragmatic, I've always been a bit superstitious, and with the September 11th tragedy in the very near past, I took this number as a bad omen. It crossed my mind that it might be a prudent idea to spend the night at the motel…but I dismissed the notion without mentioning it to Pa, in case he'd think I was being neurotic.

We drove off into the night, and by the time we were traveling down Highway 40, on the remnants of what used to be Route 66, we were both in hysterics, regaling each other with crazy teenage stories about getting wasted on Quaaludes and Boone's Farm at house parties with absent parents, making out for hours, accompanied by Led Zeppelin's "Stairway To Heaven".

The highway was utterly deserted- we were the only vehicle on the road. It was also unlit and in the pitch dark, the sky was full of stars so bright you could see them clearly through the cracked, bug-splattered windshield.

Presently, down the road in front of us, we saw a dim radiant glow, this lead to a conversation about UFO sightings. As we drew closer to the light, we realized it was coming from a gigantic truck that was spraying insecticide into the scrubby trees on the side of the road. The poisonous mist formed a large cloud, illuminated by the truck's headlights as we drove past. I told Pa about Jayne Mansfield's grisly, untimely death in Mississippi on Highway 90, when a tractor trailer swerved to avoid a mosquito spraying truck, then suddenly, we heard sirens.

I'd actually noticed the parked cop car on the side of the road earlier, and assumed it had been accompanying the spraying truck, but the moment the red and blue lights began flashing, we both realized we were getting pulled over. Since we weren't speeding, we were unsure what this was about.

Pa stopped the truck up on the shoulder and pulled out his license, instructing me to grab the registration from the glove box. The cop took his time ambling up to our truck. The moment he shined his flashlight into the cab, he saw my nurse's hat fall out of the glove compartment.

"Ma'am, " he said, "Are you a nurse?"

Staring at the cap on the floor mat with the crooked, lipstick red vinyl cross sloppily glue-gunned to it, I mumbled in real embarrassment,

"Um...no sir... I'm not a nurse."

The hat, of course, went with my bag full of slutty undies.

Shit! I thought, why *did I ignore that 911 gas pump? We should've stayed in Kingman!*

The cop directed his gaze at Pa.

"You know your license plate light is out?" he asked, as though it was a major felony.

He made both of us hand over our identification and took his sweet time calling it in. I watched the minutes ticking by on the dash clock- which miraculously, still worked- as we listened to the static dispatch radio from the squad car. Finally, the officer returned, handing us both back our licenses. He said in a monotone,

"Sir? Could you please step out of the truck?"

The moment James obliged, the cop swiftly bent him over the hood of the truck, clasping a set of cuffs on him with a loud clatter. I was halfway out of the truck's passenger door, already yelling, when the cop barked at me to "sit tight" and ordered me to "shut up for my own good". I watched mutely from the cab as he attached leg irons and a waist-chain linking them to Pa's handcuffs. By the time the pig pulled his cruiser up, throwing Pa into the back seat and slamming the door, I was out of the truck.

"What are you *doing?*" I demanded, really agitated, "What's going on?"

"I'm taking him in," the cop said, deadpan.

I was beginning to shake uncontrollably; I didn't understand what was happening, but I instinctively knew it was bad...*really bad.*

"Where are you taking him?" I shouted, starting to lose it.

"*Why* are you taking him?"

In an almost bored voice, the cop told me I really didn't need to know *why* James was getting brought in, but that they were going to the jail in

Prescott, Arizona, which was about an hour away. I could call the jail in two hours to find out the booking status.

The cop started getting into his car and abruptly, in spite of my emotional upset, my self-preservation instinct kicked in and my mind began to race: How *the hell could I call the jail when I didn't own a cell phone? Even if I had one, it wouldn't work out here...It would be completely impossible for me drive this jalopy for hours across the desert!*

Without even realizing what I was doing, I practically jumped onto the cop, blocking him from the driver's seat.

"You can't just *leave* me here," I wailed.

"By law, ma'am, I can" he said coldly.

"Call me a tow-truck," I shrieked, "You cannot leave me in the middle of nowhere at this hour!"

"Ma'am, I don't need to do that... we are leaving-*now!*" he said adamantly.

A potent adrenalin rush engulfed me so completely that I felt like I was outside myself. Suddenly I grabbed the cop roughly by the shoulders, and, in a voice I didn't even recognize as my own, got right up into his face all wild-eyed, and growled,

"Give me your *fucking* badge number then, because when they discover me raped and murdered out here, *it's gonna be in my fucking pocket!*"

The cop stared in shock as I sprawled across the hood of the police car, gripping the open door of the drive's side, preventing him from entering, screaming over and over like a banshee,

"CALL ME A TOW TRUCK NOW!"

Realizing he couldn't go anywhere without the situation escalating even more than it already had, the cop got on the radio and called a wrecker.

When he informed me that it would take around forty five minutes to arrive, I went ballistic again, yelling like a maniac that he had to wait for me because there was *no way I* could be left in the desert alone. My screams echoed into the empty night like a funhouse soundtrack. Rolling his eyes, the officer radioed for another officer to come and wait with me for the tow-truck. The cop wouldn't let me near James, not even to speak to him. I watched him forlornly through the window in the back of the squad car. The moonlight lit up the tears welling in his eyes as he mouthed to me *I'm sorry*. With that, I burst into hysterical sobs.

After what seemed like ages, the other cop arrived, oddly enough with his teenage son in tow. He stepped out of his car so both officers could have a conference. By this time, I was leaning against the back bumper of Pa's truck, tears rolling silently and steadily down my cheeks, my whole body heaving and trembling as I stared directly into the headlights of the second black and white. The lamps seemed to be dimming and getting brighter rhythmically, matching my jagged, uneven breathing. At first I thought this was an optical illusion caused by the tears from my eyes...then the squad car's motor died.

I realized, with the deep sense of dread I always got when this sort of thing happened, that it was My Electrical Disturbance leaping into action. This might be hard for some people to comprehend, but My Electrical Disturbance has plagued my entire life. I routinely freeze computers, fry cell phones, disable cameras and cash registers, go through car batteries at the rate of, like, six a year, demagnetize credit cards and can't wear a watch. My Electrical Disturbance only seems to occur when I'm extremely upset, really stressed out or very excited. When it starts happening, it scares me; I always experience even *more* anxiety and want to vomit. For years I tried to keep it a secret, but it got to the point that everyone around me started noticing. Thanks to Steven King, my close friends started calling me "Carrie" and "Firestarter".

Ultimately, I found out that the strange affliction I have is called EPK or Electro Psycho-Kinesis. It is a phenomenon that hasn't been studied much, because like me, the people who are "gifted" with it only experience it in times of extreme emotional highs or lows; generally, these actions cannot be reproduced at will, so it is impossible for researchers to collect much data on the subject.

The onset of My Electrical Disturbance was upset me even more, but I snapped back into reality when I heard both cops arguing about the dead squad car.

"But I had it serviced this morning!" The second officer was exclaiming in frustration, "Look in the log book! I checked *everything!*"

The tow truck, a huge red vintage flatbed, arrived. The driver jumped out, and in the midst of my breakdown, I noticed that with his shaggy hair, five o'clock shadow and hulking frame, he looked like a cross between Chuck Norris in the '70's and Sasquatch. After a pow wow

with the cops, he hooked our dilapidated truck to the tow bar as the car with Pa in it took off swiftly, veering off the road and across the desert in a vortex of dust, headed for Prescott.

"Get in," the tow truck driver said to me, tilting his head towards the wrecker's cab before hollering over his shoulder to the second cop and his son,

"I'll be back for you guys in about an hour!"

As we drove in silence, I tried valiantly not to bawl out loud.

"Rough night, huh?" The driver asked in a voice that was gruff but compassionate.

I couldn't answer, so he wordlessly handed me some tissues.

Finally, we pulled into what seemed to be a very small town. The driver stopped in front of a squatty cement structure with a large neon sign depicting a panther- The World Famous Black Cat Bar. Jumping out of the truck, he undid a giant padlock in the middle of a Cyclone fence and swung open the gate to his tow yard, declaring,

"We're at the end of the line, hon! Welcome to Seligman, Arizona, population 456!", he continued:

"There's a motel across the street, you can spend the night there. I charge $25.00 a day for vehicle storage up front...but you can just give it to me in the morning."

I decided that *now* wasn't the time tell him that I didn't have a credit card on me and was carrying only $28.00 in cash.

Grabbing my stuff from Pa's pickup, I crossed the deserted street and composing myself, checked into the Supai Motel, trying to ignore the fluorescent buzz of a burned out light- and the judgmental stink-eye the Indian desk clerk was giving me. I got the last room they had for $16.00...and of *course* it was Number 13. It was Spartan, with indoor-outdoor carpeting, but at least it was clean.

Momentarily I thought of visiting The World Famous Black Cat Bar and getting shit-faced with my last twelve dollars. But at the rate things were going it seemed like a horrible idea. Besides, I had other stuff to attend to... like using the old-school dial phone in the room to call the Prescott jail to check on Pa's booking and getting in touch with my sister so she

could wire me some money. I became engulfed in a gigantic shame spiral. I seriously could not *believe* this chain of events was happening to me at the age of forty-three... *Wasn't this shit supposed to magically fall away some time during the early twenties?*

And then there was the last task, one I really wasn't looking forward to at all; introducing myself *–for the very first time–* to Pa's mother via a frantic collect call at 1:45am. Gritting my teeth and steeling myself for the worst, I dialed her number.

Hello, is this Betty? My name is Pleasant. You don't know me, but I'm your son's girlfriend. Sorry to wake you up, but I'm stranded somewhere in the middle of Arizona, and James is in jail...

Pa had already processed through the Yavapai County Jail in Prescott, but the only information I could get besides the fact that they were holding him without bail and wouldn't let me speak to him. My sister wasn't home so I left a message. The phone call with Pa's mom went, I suppose, as well as a phone call of that nature could possibly go...at least she didn't hang up on me.

By then, it was 2:25 am, too late for The Black Cat, and I sure as hell couldn't sleep. All there was left to do was chain smoke, cry, and maybe try to numb myself by watching TV. The ancient television, with its rabbit-ear antenna, took a long time to tune in, but when the picture finally materialized showing the Channel 10 station identification logo, the announcer's deep voice boomed:

WE NOW RETURN YOU TO OUR MOVIE *CHINATOWN*, STARRING JACK NICHOLSON AND FAYE DUNAWAY.

The film flickered onto to the screen at the very point where the "My sister.... My daughter" scene began.

All the hair on my body stood on end. I shuddered in utter disbelief, chills running up my spine. I felt like I was drowning, like my brain was being sucked slowly and loudly out of my skull. In the midst of it all, my thoughts came thick and fast.

How was this even possible...especially after the episode with My Electrical Disturbance? Why the hell hadn't I paid attention to that damn gas pump? More importantly, how come my clairvoyance had shown me "Chinatown", and not the part about the police pulling us over? What the fuck?

I started crying hysterically again, and at some point, still in my clothing, fell into a deep, fitful sleep. I awoke to blinding desert sunlight and the tinny sounds of ranchera music on a cheap radio, floating above the roar of the maid's vacuum cleaner in the room next door. I took a shower and tried to apply make-up over my tear-swollen eyes. I was gonna need every bit of what was left of my feminine wiles to figure out storing the truck, not to mention getting out of Seligman, considering the fact that I was twelve bucks away from being flat broke. Grabbing a paper cup full of the brown crayon water that was masquerading as coffee in the lobby, I began trying to think coherently about negotiating vehicle storage at the tow yard.

The Chuck Norris guy greeted me brusquely with a grunt as I entered his garage. He rolled out from beneath the chassis, dressed in worn, grease-stained coveralls. Lighting a Marlboro, he repeated his terms, and then asked if my boyfriend had gotten out of jail. I started weeping as I recounted the previous nights events...leaving out the crazy paranormal shit so I wouldn't sound completely insane.

"Oh, man...*please* don't cry!" he begged, his demeanor changing unexpectedly,

"I just cannot handle seeing a woman cry!"

He gestured for me to sit down on a plastic orange crate as he handed me a glass of water and a clean red chamois cloth to wipe my eyes with.

"You seem like a nice person, " he said earnestly, " I know you're really upset...and I'm not sure why your boyfriend is in jail..."

"I'm not either!" I wailed, lips quivering, snot bubbling out of my nostrils like a child, "They wouldn't *tell* me!"

He looked me straight in the eyes and told me he would store the truck until James got out of jail, and only charge me five bucks a day instead twenty five, but that I had to promise to mail him the cash as soon as I got home. Gratefully agreeing to his terms, I offered to leave my license as collateral, but he waved his hand in dismissal. Writing up a receipt, he said a Greyhound bus came through the town and let me use the shop phone to make a reservation. The automated voice stated that the bus only stopped in Seligman every three days; apparently, I'd just missed one. Seligman, known as "The Birthplace of Route 66" is situated in Northern Arizona's Upland Mountains, "conveniently located" exactly 180 miles away from both Phoenix and The Grand Canyon...which was actually a euphemism for *In The Middle Of Nowhere.*

As I hung up in despair, the tow driver told me I could get a flight from Flagstaff to Phoenix, so I could then fly to LA. I reached my sister, told her the predicament, and she called back after she'd booked the flights for me. Wolfing down the Snickers bar the tow guy offered me after he called the taxi service, I thanked him gratefully and profusely for his kindness. Things were actually starting to look up!

The cab, which turned out to be a black 1980's Cadillac Seville with a burgundy velvet interior, arrived an hour and change later. The sunburned driver was portly in a plaid shirt; Polyester pants and a shocking white comb-over. Holding the door open for me, he stated that the journey to Flagstaff would take roughly two hours. Shaking Chuck Norris' hand, I stepped into the car's front seat and we took off.

Neil Diamond was playing softly on the radio as we drove through the barren desert. Thinking of Pa in jail, I felt tears welling up again. Staring out the window at the scrubby landscape, I tried to be as silent as possible, just for the sake of being polite.

An hour or so went by before the cabbie, in a timid voice, ventured,

"Miss? I know this isn't any of my business, and I don't know what happened to you, but I hope you'll be all right... I don't want to pry... but..."

Taking a measured breath, he continued,

" I wanted to let you know that... you're... the most beautiful woman I've ever had in my cab. I'm a married man, so I don't... *mean anything* by this...but I want to help, so... this ride is on me".

I looked over at his sincere face and burst into tears again, this time, because of a total stranger's compassion.

"Thank you so much!" I sobbed.

We drove the rest of the way in silence. When he let me out at the Flagstaff Airport he wouldn't take a tip, just patted me on the arm in a fatherly way and wished me luck. Even though the airport was the size of a postage stamp with only one runway, because the September 11th

tragedy had was still a brand new, open wound, the security line was a bitch. As it happened, I had a "starred ticket", which meant I was singled out for "secondary search". The extremely thorough agents succeeded in knocking six keys off my brand new laptop. Then they confiscated all the vintage diaper pins inside my bag. *Like, sure, I was totally planning to hi-jack the plane by brandishing a diaper pin decorated with a yellow plastic ducky!* As they did this, a woman breezed through the line wearing one of those giant American Flag pins made of beads- and twenty or thirty safety pins.

"What about *her*? " I asked indignantly. "She's got tons of safety pins on!"

"Oh, " the security agent said, "That's *just jewelry!*"

With all the procedures, I barely made my plane, which turned out to be a single-engine eight seater. Five passengers were men, ranging from executives to desert rats, and there was a pair of newly weds who'd obviously been honeymooning at the Grand Canyon. Their affection made me lonely for Pa and their clean-cut appearance made me envious. It was clear that neither of them had never jumped on the hood of a police car screaming like a lunatic, experienced psychic issues involving popular films, or gotten stranded in a surreal one-horse town with no money. I felt immensely sorry for myself and during the bumpy take off, the crying kicked in again.

I didn't even notice the incredible turbulence until the flight attendant started doling out barf bags to everyone- handing mine to me along with small package of Kleenex. As we flew directly into a vicious thunderstorm, the plane hurdled up and shot down hundreds of feet like a thrill ride. Shell shocked, I watched with a detached fascination as huge, fake-looking white bolts of lightning practically bounced off the wings. Passengers were heaving loudly and the entire cabin reeked of vomit. The new bride clutched her husband's hand praying out loud and the pilot yelled frantically into his headset as the flight attendant white-knuckled her seat.

After what seemed like forever, the plane burst out of the storm and into glaring sunlight, making an abrupt descent into Phoenix. Everyone filed off the plane and onto the tarmac like zombies.

Since I had an hour to kill- and had almost died- I found the closest bar right away. Gulping down two shots of vodka in quick succession, I noticed the woman on the stool next to me staring...*I'm a fucking wreck.*

She looked like a Casino Trash Bingo Lady from Laughlin who'd been a stripper in her youth, with her fried blonde hair and sun damaged skin covered in harsh, cheap make up.

"Been there, done that, got the T-shirt", she said with a kind, knowing expression crossing her weathered face.

"Your drinks are on me!" she stated firmly, ordering me another shot.

I don't remember the flight back to LA, or getting home. As soon as I did, I called Prescott and learned that Pa had been transferred to The Yavapai County Detention Facility. I waited through a series of automated prompts and recordings before I got a human being. At first, the CO wouldn't let me talk to James or leave a message, explaining that inmates couldn't receive messages unless there was a Verified Emergency Situation. After I called back six or seven times in quick succession pretending to be a pregnant spouse who was going into labor, in exasperation the guy finally said he'd give my husband the message and allow him to place a collect call to me.

Half an hour later, I gladly accepted the charges, rejoicing in hearing Pa's voice. He sounded ok in spite of everything he'd been through: getting shackled with the "4-piece" – the cuffs and chain arrangement usually reserved for serial killers- while sitting in the back of a squad car and then waiting for an hour on a bench in Prescott waiting to get processed. He'd gone to jail in ancient shredded jeans and a T-shirt emblazoned with a ventriloquist dummy with a bloody Manson X on its forehead and "Puppet Terror" written beneath it in drippy horror movie letters. He didn't have a cent on him and was barefoot, so he was booked as an "indigent". He still hadn't found out why he was being held or when he'd be released. I promised to wire cash to be put into his commissary account and we phone-kissed. The call ended far too quickly, but reassured that my lover wasn't being mistreated, I slept peacefully for just over twenty-four hours.

The next couple of days were filled with calls to his mother (who, not surprisingly, was cautious and suspicious each time we spoke) and cyber-stalking the Yavapai County Detention Center to the point that I knew how many employees they had and all about the new prison-wide plumbing system they were installing.

In a couple more days, Pa finally found out why he was being detained. It turned out that a court summons had erroneously been sent to an address at which he hadn't lived at for *years*. Eventually it turned into a bench warrant, and the recent passing of the Patriot Act had qualified

any "fugitives from justice" to be extradited back to the state they'd fled for trial and/or punishment. So Pa was held in custody in Arizona until New Mexico sent for his transport, which would land him in the Santa Fe County Adult Correctional Center until his trial. We'd *definitely* need a criminal lawyer to unravel this mess, even though it stemmed from a clerical error. I was at an absolute loss at how to find a competent attorney in another state. There were dozens of them listed, but trying to actually reach one on the phone was impossible. Either the lawyers were "busy" and I'd be forced speak to a clueless paralegal who didn't understand the situation and apparently never left a message, or it was suggested I come to New Mexico for a consultation- yeah, *right!* And then I remembered Mr. V.

I'd known Mr. V for years- he'd gone to school with one of my sisters. Somehow during a boozy party at her place, Mr. V had pegged me as a libertine, and pulled me aside to confidentially ask me for sexual advice regarding his current girlfriend. Evidently, I counseled him quite well, because he began calling me every few months to ask my take on stuff like getting a girl to role-play or how to introduce light bondage into a relationship. These calls became regular, like, every time he had a date - and he was dating a *lot*- but they were clean and clinical as opposed to kinky. I didn't feel creeped out at all, but I *was* starting to feel like an unpaid sex therapist! When he called for the third time in one week, wondering about coercing his latest fling into getting spanked, I joked that he would have to repay me someday. Since Mr. V was a former state senator who was currently a lawyer, that time was *now*.

As luck would have it, Mr. V was happy to reciprocate, hooking me up with a man who was supposed to be the best criminal defense attorney in the Southwest; he even wrote a personal letter of recommendation. The lawyer took the case, but the court date wouldn't be set until Pa was extradited back to New Mexico.

Meantime, James seemed to be having a fine time in the Detention Center, as detailed in his many letters to me. Along with heartfelt passages about how much he missed me, he wrote descriptions of day-to-day prison life. Apparently, because I was still calling constantly to check on his status, I'd become something of a celebrity among the correctional officers. During the Lights Out rounds, while dragging his baton along the metal bars, one of them had even taken to clandestinely whispering out of the side of his mouth, "Packard- your wife called again!"

His correspondence described all the various inmate cliques: the Mexicans who'd lift weights by attaching plastic trash bags full of water to each side of a broomstick, the trannies who offered hair cuts to other inmates from their cell-salons, the Meth freaks and the White Power guys. He wrote about the shitty food and the people who served it. The prison had separate buildings for men and women in the same compound, and the food-serving trustees worked both sides. For a price, they'd smuggle foil-wrapped notes -hidden under the lid of the meal plastic containers- back and forth between lovers who resided in different cell blocks. One letter of Pa's included pencil rubbings of the tweaker graffiti carved into the metal benches, another was written from the viewpoint of an ET who'd somehow gotten incarcerated.

Through the grapevine, James learned that many of the inmates believed Yavapai County was shaped like a pentagram, and that the Sheriff's office was the very center of the star. Then there was The Truth Hurts Incident. The only channel the big screen television in the common room ever played was MTV, all day and night. Pa just happened to be watching when my video made its debut. All the convicts were crowded around the television, whistling and catcalling at the hip-hop hotties shaking their booties. When I swirled onto the screen in my sparkly blue and gold costume and veils, undulating in a "private dance" for Dr. Dre, Pa proudly announced to everyone that I was his girlfriend. *Of course they all thought he was joking!*

He'd also become the star of a true Big House rags-to-riches story. Because of his artistic talent, he was now rolling in cigarettes, candy bars, Hostess Cakes, postage stamps, and Swiss Miss drink packets.... all paid to him by his fellow inmates. He was doing a roaring business drawing birthday and greeting cards to send to their mothers, wives and baby-mommas. His work was composed of intricate pencil drawings decorated with cherubs, hearts and roses colored in vivid yellows, reds and greens, using powdered Jell-O mix and water as paint. He even designed a tattoo of a raging bull for somebody and watched it get inked into the guy's skin by hand. I could practically see the headlines: *Jailhouse Indigent Makes Good!*

On the last day it was possible to extradite James from Yavapai County to the county jail in Santa Fe, the New Mexico officers showed up. They'd flown over in a Cessna to bring him back to wait for his trial.

Green-faced, one of the cops was so sick and terrified in the tiny plane that Pa wound up holding his hand the entire way.

The jail there was vastly different than in Arizona- Pa was put into General Population, which was basically a huge cage full of people who were batshit crazy. In comparison, the Yavapai Country Detention center had been a cakewalk. He kept a low profile as he waited for another two weeks for his day in court.

Apparently, Mr. V had done an absolutely bang-up job of finding us a lawyer. Though the retainer was hideously expensive, he was for real, the best criminal defense attorney in the state. He was also the presiding judge's golf buddy, and had been a mentor to the prosecuting attorney when he'd been in law school!

A few days after the trial, James returned to Hollywood in his rattletrap pick up truck. He hugged me long and tight and we kissed for eons.

"I brought you a present from jail", he said jubilantly, handing me a grocery bag and a tattered paper clipping.

Some guys learn how to crack safes or become bookies when they're on the inside; others kill their fellow inmates with shanks made from a toothbrush. But Pa had been going through magazines in Santa Fe, looking for *recipes*. The one he handed me was for Southern Fried chicken, written by Martha Stewart...a good two years before she herself was incarcerated.

"I'm starving," Pa said, getting out a frying pan, "Let's try this!"

As I handed him the contents of the grocery bag, he squeezed me and sighed regretfully,

"You know, when we were in Kingman? The gas pump price said $9.11. I didn't think that was a good sign, and I wanted to stay there at the motel...but I didn't tell you because I thought you'd think I was crazy!"

TALES OF TOURING TERROR

The year was 1985, and my crazy, liquor-soaked, thrashin' all-girl cow punk band The Screaming Sirens were on a US tour promoting our first album, *Fiesta*. We were booked into a roadhouse called Rooster's in Nashville, Tennessee and had been living like full on "Spinal Tap" style road-pigs. We'd been playing every night and- *if we were lucky*-sleeping on stranger's floors. Our unheated old Winnebago conversion van, which we called The Pupa, wasn't air-conditioned and the heater didn't work that well, so no matter what the season, it was always uncomfortable. The ceiling was festooned with fishnet stockings, crepe paper streamers, bumper stickers, and our own lipstick graffiti. The windows on one side were plastered with torn-apart Tampax boxes, to block out the sun...and to act as a warning to all the hapless college radio fans who came to our shows, that five batshit crazy women were inside, their monthly cycles neatly synced up.

This story unfolds on the eve of Sirens' bassist Laura's birthday, on a chilly November night.

As twilight fell, I stepped outside the stage door of Rooster's and as my eyes became accustomed to the dim light, I couldn't believe what I was seeing...a mossy Victorian-era gravestone, leaning up against the building, almost covered in weeds. There was new dirt and clumps of grass stuck to the bottom of the monument; it looked to be freshly dug up. Even more amazing, the headstone was for a girl who had died at age twenty-four: the same age Laura was turning that very night. Not only that, the girl had died on November 4th... *Laura's birthday!* Going inside the club to report my find, I asked if there was a graveyard anywhere in the nearby vicinity. Everyone I asked from the club assured me there was not.

Thinking the headstone would make the ultimate birthday present, I borrowed a hand-truck from the club and cajoled some local boys to help get the headstone to our dressing room. Blindfolding Laura, I dragged her inside to see her present. She was my partner in crime- a tough, hard-drinking, wisecracking punk chick, who, before joining the Sirens, had been in a band called Hard As Nails, Cheap As Dirt. Laura had a macabre sense of humor, and like the rest of us, always appreciated a low-budget splatter flick, so the whole band assumed she'd be *delighted* with her present...especially since we were too broke to be able to afford anything else.

As the blindfold was removed, instead of the anticipated reaction of delighted laughter, Laura turned-pun intended- white as a ghost. She whispered hoarsely, her voice trembling audibly,

"Get that fucking thing out of here right now!"

Disappointed that our gift didn't go over well as we'd thought it would, we scrambled to get the gravestone back where I'd found it, crashing into amps and drum sets in the narrow hallway on the way out. Eerily, the headstone seemed to put a curse on everything that happened after that.

Our gig that night was terrible- maybe the worst of the whole tour- plagued with much more than our usual share of technical difficulties. The boys we were flirting with didn't respond the way they usually did, the audience was a bunch of dullard cowboys and we didn't sell any merch. As we loaded up the van in a dense fog, it began to drizzle, then Laura's purse somehow disappeared from the parking lot. The whole band searched for ages both inside and outside the club as well as in our van, but it had vanished without a trace. Dead tired and with no speed or even coffee, because it was so late that even rural convenience marts and truck-stops weren't open, Laura and I drove the van through lighting, thunder and torrential rain for three and a half hours before discovering we'd gone in the wrong direction. Usually we chattered endlessly on our late-night drives, but tonight we were both quiet and grimly introspective. Practically crying, we *finally* figured out the right way to go. Back on course, we were speeding through Kentucky at daybreak, desperately trying to get to St. Louis on time for our gig that night, and then we got pulled over.

Laura was driving, and since her purse was missing, she had no license. We both looked completely terrifying in our previous night's sweat- caked stage make up. Remnants of glitter crusted around our eyes, we looked like carnival corpses from a cheap funhouse. Laura was wearing a decomposing vintage beaver fur coat over long-johns and I was a clown: orange hair with rags tied into it, a man's 1950's pajama shirt, huge torn-up net petticoat, boxer shorts, red striped stockings and turquoise Converse high-tops. Everyone else was passed out cold, and we both silently prayed the van wouldn't get searched- because if it did, we'd probably wind up on a rural chain gang!

The cop didn't even have to say *Yew ain't from 'round heeere, are ya?* We could see the diabolical inbred glint in his eyes. Miraculously, he didn't seem to notice the scores of "dead soldier" Budweiser cans that littered the floor along with stray fishnet stockings, crumpled cigarette packs, No-Doz boxes, rolling papers, battered cowboy boots and an empty bottle of Everclear.

That cop screwed us up pretty good, anyway: we not only got a seventy-five dollar ticket (an astronomical amount in those days, especially for *us*) he kept the van up at the side of the road for almost forty minutes as he made a huge deal of having his dispatcher call LA to make sure Laura didn't have any warrants. The fact that it was confirmed to be her birthday held no sway with him even though we explained our predicament-her stolen purse, and that we were a band late for a gig. Even though the road we were speeding on was completely deserted, he wrote us the ticket with sardonic glee. Finally arriving in St. Louis, we sent our entire band-fund back to LA by money order. We reasoned that because of the way things were going, we were scared to keep a large amount of cash with us, just in case it got lost or stolen. Plus, our gig that night was an anchor date with the biggest guarantee of the tour, so we'd be flush in a matter of hours.

When we got to the club, we found out that the booking agent who'd hired us had apparently been fired recently. The club's manager was like, "Screaming *who?*"

We sat in the parking lot forlornly, with grim reality setting in. We had only sixty-odd dollars left to share between seven people-counting our personal monetary stashes- and no gig for three days. As it began to snow, we made repeated attempts to contact the promoter of the next show in Kansas City by pay phone, but no dice. Boy, were we *bummed.*

Pretty soon, the guys in the Top Forty house band showed up for their gig that night. They'd found out from the club's manager that we were a stranded all-girl band from LA, and, interest piqued, they smuggled beer and popcorn out to us. We shared our last shreds of pot and recited our tale of woe.

The house band guys excitedly told us that Supertramp was playing the coliseum down the street and that the after-party was being held here at the club...*like we cared!* Supertramp? You gotta be kidding! We were so Alternative that we had no idea what Supertramp's hits were, and didn't give a shit anyway. But those Top Forty guys were being nice to us... so we were nice right back, acting suitably, charmingly impressed with this "amazing" news.

We borrowed a couple of bucks from them and went out to an absolutely dismal Italian birthday dinner at The Spaghetti Factory. All of us shared plates of food, drinking communally from the decanter of hellish, vinegary cheap red wine. Laura blew out her one candle and we all split the pathetically stale chocolate cup cake as though it was manna from heaven. We barely had enough to pay the bill and left someone's keychain and a random punk rock badge as a tip.

We drove back to the club's parking lot -*where else were we gonna go*- and since it was really starting to blizzard by now and we didn't want to risk driving or running out of gas in a snow storm, figured that we'd spend the night right there in the parking lot, shivering in our unheated van. On cue, the Top Forty guys came out again with more beer and we joked around. Even though they were "normal" and we were punk rock scum, we were still chicks, and *chick musicians,* no less… which really was a novelty in those days. They were intrigued with us, because even though we were broke and stranded, we were living out a rock 'n' roll dream, and besides, we were from *Hollywood!*

The guys went inside and convinced the manager to let us play a set on their equipment. They were insanely delighted when we emerged from the club's bathroom, looking all fresh and newly made-up with our garish Ronnettes-style eyeliner and Wet 'N' Wild ninety-nine cent lipstick. I have to say that through the wonders of Aqua Net and dime store make up we always cleaned up *very* well…even on tour with hangovers and no showers. The Top Forty guys kept bringing us pitchers of beer before we went on, and while they played, they announced to the entire club that it was Laura's birthday, and told our whole sad, crazy story onstage.

Pretty soon the entire club sang "Happy Birthday" out loud to Laura. We played a wild set, with audience members sending trays of shots up onto the stage. Construction workers in plaid shirts were jumping right up onto the stage to shake our hands, steal a kiss or do a shot with us. The audience was going crazy cause they'd never seen five girls in torn-up lingerie and biker jackets jumping around, sweating, cursing and actually playing well.

When we finished, the guys from Supertramp congratulated us, buying rounds of cocktails and giving us tons of blow in the dressing room, yelling in practically unintelligible English accents about how *Fakkin' Greht* we were. During their set, in between every song, they took up a cash collection from the audience so we could have gas money. We'd played with a wild assortment of bands in our career, from The Ramones to Roseanne Cash, but never once dreamed we'd *ever* open for Supertramp!

40

By the end of the night, our luck had turned around. Our roadie Jonny Lee had gotten in touch with the promoter in Kansas City, who'd arranged for us to stay that night at his mom's house; soft beds, showers, home-cooked meals and cable television... *yeee-haw*!

It's beenabout three decades, but to this day, if you mention the word *birthday* to Laura, she winces in pain and changes the subject right away.

THE WILDEST RIDES OF 2011

I spent most of 2011 on the road, which wasn't much of a change from most previous years. Though I could definitely live without the scary airport food and the hassle of condensing my cosmetics in a TSA-approved quart baggie, I love most aspects of traveling. To this day, I feel blessed grateful that I'm not only doing something I love-performing and teaching dance- but that I get to travel all over the world to do it! But life on the road isn't always glamorous as you might think... I often joke that every year, I lose at least fifty IQ points to jetlag!

Traveling seems to generate unusual incidents, at least for *me* it does. I've been through six separate hotel fires: Vancouver, BC; Memphis Tennessee (those two were a week apart!) at The Flamingo in Las Vegas, twice on board the Queen Mary in Long Beach, California, and at the Mena House Oberoi in Cairo. I've missed countless planes and had my suitcase handle break off on an English train platform... while the train departed *and my suitcase remained at the station!*

I've been delayed and searched at international borders, gotten so spectacularly stoned on hash in Amsterdam that I seriously thought I was going to die, been left by a lover in Paris, and spent the night in a Cairo police station. I bump into all sorts of random people at airports, including rock stars. Ron Wood from The Stones helped me get my bags off the carousel in Chicago, and I walked right into Alice Cooper at the airport in Athens, Greece. I see people I know in foreign places, too. On a flight from Heathrow to Los Angeles, I endured an awful thunderstorm with infamous LA punk band manager and record magnate Posh Boy, and on a return flight from Egypt that transferred through Paris I was coincidentally booked on the same plane to LAX as my ex-husband!

Beyond that, once in a while, it gets even wackier. Often it's just a matter of not understanding the language or confusion over local customs, but other times things get so totally out of hand and downright *bizarre* that I actually start to think: *There's the signpost up ahead...The Twilight Zone!*

In 2011, I was in five different countries before Valentine's Day, and wasn't home longer than a week and a half until just before Christmas. As per usual, I spent a lot of that travel time on a bullet train to Crazy Town.

In February 2011, I went on a solo European dance tour. Not only did my luggage get lost three times on flights to three different countries, but also the two and a half hour ferryboat ride from Helsinki, Finland to Tallinn, Estonia was completely surreal.

To begin with, Finland and Estonia are so far north that in February, it doesn't get light til about 10:00 am, and darkness sets in again a little after 3:00 pm. That alone is disorienting to a California Sunshine Gal like me. The median temperature while I was there, was *28 degrees below zero*. My nostrils literally froze and my eyes ached every time I went outside. I don't know how those Northern gals look glamorous in winters like that, but they all do, trotting around on the ice in stiletto-heeled platform boots and jackets made of real fur.

The morning I was leaving Helsinki to go to Tallinn, I had to be up super early, check out of the hotel, and get to the ferry dock two hours before the ship departed at 9:00 am.... or, as I took to calling it, *dawn*. I was meeting my Estonian sponsor Berit and the other gals from her belly dance studio Mustika at the Helsinki dock, because they'd come to Finland for my workshops. In my haste, I didn't have time for breakfast, so I grabbed a hard-boiled egg from the buffet and shoved it into my purse.

The dock looked like Ellis Island it was so crowded, and I didn't know the ferry was going to be so big, it was the size of a cruise ship. The embarkation line stretched outside into the darkness and falling snow. Also, the ocean was completely *frozen*. The boats all had ice cutters on the prow and as they pulled in and out of the harbor huge chunks of ice flew up like a gigantic blender!

I finally found the Estonian girls, and we got on the ferry. It was three stories high; there was a duty free shop, a huge casino, restaurants, and lots of bars, plus a lounge area that had karaoke, where we settled. Berit said it was the best place to spend the journey, and asked if I wanted breakfast or coffee from the bar. I dug in my purse and pulled out my egg, confessing I'd had no idea there'd be food onboard.

All the Estonian dancers laughed in disbelief.

"You look like an old Russian grandma!", said Daisi, a burlesque chick from Tallinn, as Berit took off her scarf and wrapped it around my head like a *babushka,*

"What else do you have in your purse?"

The ship started sailing and the moment we had our coffee, a lounge singer came on, singing Beatles and Johnny Cash songs in Finnish, Estonian and Russian.

"Oh shit," Daisi groaned, "This is *not* helping my hangover!"

Soon the karaoke began. As Daisi winced in pain and the other girls kept joking about my egg, we were treated to hideous versions in various languages of ABBA's "Dancing Queen", Aqua's "Barbie Girl" and the enduring all-time Euro-trash hit, "Don't Worry, Be Happy".

Soon, a young, wholesome-looking guy dressed all in white, with a tousled blonde bowl-cut took the microphone, and before he started singing, everyone burst into applause. As he launched into a terrifyingly off-key rendition A-Ha's "Take On Me", the Estonian dancers started laughing hysterically and whispering amongst themselves.

"What's so funny?" I asked, confused since they were speaking Estonian.

"Oh, this man singing is the biggest porn star in Estonia!" Yahna exclaimed.

"No way!" I said, convinced they were making fun of me in all my jet lag.

"No, *really,* he is!" Daisi assured me, " Everyone knows him in Estonia, and he is very famous for his bondage and latex videos!"

As I sat dumbfounded, Berit added,

"His name is Arnold, but we call him "Second Arnold" because "First Arnold" is our president, Arnold Ruutel!"

Just before "Second Arnold" launched into Culture Club's "Do You Really Want to Hurt Me", I started to believe them, because a few audience members went up to him and had him sign autographs on napkins.

"I can't take this any more," Berit, declared, "I'm going to Duty Free."

When she returned, Second Arnold was still hogging the mic. He was on his sixth song, much to the delight of the crowd. Some matronly older women practically stormed the stage giggling like schoolgirls, taking pictures.

"I got you something to go with your egg!" Berit cried, handing me a foot-long plastic sperm, with big googley cartoon eyes.

As Second Arnold began to croon Duran Duran's, "Hungry Like The Wolf", I held the giant sperm in my hand, regarding it mutely, quite unsure of reality at this point.

"Some *cream* for your coffee!" Yahna laughed, as Berit unscrewed the sperm's head and poured a whitish-yellow substance out of its body and into my cup.

As I stared in shock, Berit assured me it was Bailey's Irish Crème… and, thankfully it really was!

Arnold didn't stop singing for the rest of the voyage.

*   *   *

It's June 2011, and I'm in Cairo, which is curiously quiet and sedate due to the social unrest that has plagued Egypt for most of the Arab Spring. There are practically no tourists anywhere, and The Ahlan Wa Sahlan Belly Dance Festival has only about 200 attendees, as opposed to almost 1,500 the year before. My jet lag has grown to new proportions, as it always does by mid-year. I am no longer sure what time it is *anywhere*. The jetlag to Egypt is always really bad, but this year, it seems worse. I literally haven't slept in three days.

So, I'm talking to a really nice lady about buying a traditional Egyptian *gallibayya* dress. She has a beautiful, friendly looking face, and her hijab or head scarf perfectly matches the pink bowling shirt – embroidered with a huge Betty Boop- that she is wearing over her own *gallibaya*.

The woman speaks English very well, and I'm trying to stay focused on the conversation, but I'm so spun out from lack of sleep, my eyes keep drifting from her face to her shirt. There's English writing on it, but as she moves around, unfolding garments for me to look at, I can't see exactly what it says. Eventually, I sort of make out the slogan…*and it seems to me like something a crack whore would be wearing in a Laughlin, Nevada trailer park.* I remind myself that I am, in fact, in Cairo, and there's no way in hell this gracious Egyptian woman would be wearing a shirt with an obscene joke on it.

Finally, after I've paid for the *gallibaya* I'm purchasing, she stands still for a second, and I realize that her shirt indeed says *exactly* what I think it says:

IF YOU'RE GONNA RIDE MY ASS, AT LEAST PULL MY HAIR

I can't stop staring in total amazement, it's as though I'm hypnotized... and then she notices me looking.

"Uh.... I like your shirt," I manage lamely.

"Oh yes!" She says enthusiastically, pointing to Betty Boop and practically yelling,

"I am so love cartoon!"

Suddenly, I realize she has absolutely *no idea* what her shirt says...and apparently nobody else does, either... otherwise she definitely wouldn't be wearing it! I tell her that her English is very good, and ask her if she reads English as well as speaking it. She shakes her head no.

"What it says?" she asks me, as if on cue, "Read shirt to me!"

Since her hair is covered, I know she is religious. If I tell her what the shirt really says, she will be absolutely humiliated...*beyond* humiliated. I think there's a good chance she will run to the bathroom crying hysterically, lock herself inside and never come out. I don't want to embarrass her in any way, but I can't think of anything to substitute for what is written on her shirt, and I'm panicking.

Finally, I come up with a solution. I ask if she's married. When the answer is affirmative, I know it's safe to say to her,

"I can't tell you exactly what your shirt says, but in America, this shirt is very funny...and..."I let my voice drop to a confidential whisper,

"Well...it's also a little bit *sexy!*"

"Oooh!" She gasps in scandalous delight, her eyes widen and her hand flies up to her mouth as she chortles conspiratorially,

"I like very much sexy!"

Since she has made a good sale, we've had a nice glass of tea together and now, we are both laughing out loud, she insists that we take a picture together...so of course, we do.

*   *   *

It's September 2011 and I'm furiously preparing for The Las Vegas Belly Dance Intensive. Not only am I performing and teaching at the event, my brand new line of Egyptian-made belly dance costumes- Princess Farhana For King Of The Nile- will be making it's debut there, in three separate fashion shows. I've spent the past two and a half months on Skype to Cairo with my partner for hours every day, approving designs and seeing finished products. I'm also going crazy trying via email to corral my models- fourteen belly dancers from seven different states- to pin down their availability for the fashion shows. My partner emails that he's sent the costume boxes from Egypt, but when I try to track them, all that comes up is a notice saying:

ALL DELIVERIES DELAYED INDEFINITELY DUE TO HURRICANE IRENE

I try to breathe evenly and ignore my impending sense of doom, but I can't help it.

A few days later, my partner arrives in America and the tracking shows that the boxes arrived.... *Thank God!*

All is going well until the Friday of Labor Day weekend, when I somehow re-injure my neck. Two years previously, I was in my car at a full stop when an SUV plowed into my vehicle, resulting in my suffering severe whiplash and six- *yes, six*- herniated discs. During my extensive treatment and healing process, my doctors had warned me that my spine would "never be the same", and that sometimes, the "jelly" inside the disc might bulge out and create discomfort.

Well, I'm here to tell you that I have never, *ever*, experienced pain like this before, not even when the accident had first occurred! I call every doctor I can, but because it's a holiday weekend, nobody is in. I begin icing immediately, swallow insane amounts of ibuprophen and pacing constantly like a lunatic, because the pain is so intense, it feels like there are electric screwdrivers in my neck and blowtorches on my shoulder I can't sit or sleep, and I'm moaning and keening out loud like a wild animal that's just been shot. It's a monumental pain, I want to die. This goes on all weekend long.

Monday is Labor Day, and it's Tuesday morning before any of my doctors call me back.

The doctor diagnoses me with a cervical disc that is bulging onto my nerve channels and sets me up with steroids and a new pain medication that I'd never had before. I take it and feel sweet relief... *Finally!* After taking the second dose a few hours later, I feel almost normal, and decide to pack for Vegas, since I was leaving the very next day. I don't realize how high I am, because I'm literally *feeling no pain.* Halfway through packing, I trip over my suitcase, fly across the room and land in a heap on my floor. Laughing like a crazed junkie, I just continue to pack. Two hours later, I wonder why my foot still hurts. Looking down, I realize I've broken the last two toes on my right foot. Now, I've broken toes before, and the most a doctor can do is tape them up, and I certainly wasn't going to a doctor again! I stare in amazement at their shiny purple hue, all fat and swollen. I eat another pill, swallow an airline-sized bottle of vodka, and gritting my teeth, yank both toes back into their regular positions. Still high, I photograph my foot and post it on Twitter before taping up the toes and continuing to pack.

The next morning I leave for Vegas, and from the moment I'm there, it's crackers. The fashion shows go great, and my show with Arabic band House Of Tarab goes pretty well too, considering I was hardly putting any weight on my right foot! I don't know what I would've done without my dear friend DeVilla, who came to model for me, but winds up being my personal assistant all weekend.

My workshop is another story entirely. I knew I could teach with my neck jacked up - I'd done it when I was healing from the accident, after all- so that wasn't a problem. But the broken toes kind of throw a wrench in the matter of doing floor work, which was one of the advertised aspects of the workshop... and since I broke my toes the day before I left, and I was going to be at the Intensive anyway, I thought it would be idiotic to cancel the class.

I explain this turn of events to the forty or so students, hoping they'll understand, and have DeVilla come up on stage with me to be my demo-model. As soon as I start warming up, breathing in and out, all the lights in the ballroom begin dimming and coming up, in rhythm with breathing and the way my arms raise and fall. At first, I don't think anything of this because I often have weird experiences with electricity- until all the lights go completely off and come up a few times, strobing like disco lights. This goes on non-stop for a few minutes.... like, ten minutes! By now I'm completely distracted, and the whole class is murmuring and making jokes about it, too.

My Electrical Disturbance has been with me since childhood. Cell phones and computers fail regularly, I can make my television turn on and off with a wave of my hand, I cause streetlights to go out when I walk beneath them, and light bulbs sometimes actually explode as I go past. This usually happens in times of stress...and I guess my stress has reached a head by now.

"What's up with the lights?" I yell across the room to one of the festival volunteers.

"I don't know," she hollers back, "They've been fine all day and there were four classes in here!"

Great!

DeVilla pushes me out of the way, steps up to the mic and regales the workshop attendees with stories of my "super powers", and recounts how many crazy electrical incidents she's personally witnessed during the numerous times we've traveled together. She's telling so many stories from so many places I'm beginning to get really embarrassed... it's not like I can *control* this "talent" I have. The lights ultimately settle down, and we get on with the class.

For the rest of the trip, DeVilla receives her "punishment" for blabbing about my electrical secrets. Poor girl, she'd anticipated a weekend of modeling, gambling, and laying poolside with a margarita in hand, but instead she has to play Nurse Maid. She makes sure I take my pills, she brings me ice, tapes up my toes daily and changes the Lidocaine pain patches on the back of my left shoulder every few hours. I couldn't have done that weekend without her- I owe her *big time*.

And if you happened to be in my class at The Intensive that year, now you know why it was so cray-cray!

*   *   *

It's November 2011 and I'm doing a couple of dates in the Midwest - Kansas and Missouri, to be exact. I love the Midwest, and I've been there a lot. America's heartland is beautiful, laid back and calm compared to Los Angeles and a lot of the other places I go. The dancers are always a lot of fun, and I look forward to my workshops there, because I can always be assured of a calm, peaceful trip.

Not this time!

The Manhattan, Kansas-based belly dance troupe, Eyes Of Bastet, are sponsoring me for my second-to-last trip of the year. Cathia, Nashid and I had a long, laughter-filled ride from the airport, a great barbecue dinner where I met the rest of their lovely troupe, and I'm now ensconced in my really plush hotel room, more modern and higher-end than most places I've stayed at in major cities. I sink gratefully into my Tempur-pedic hotel bed and I'm on the brink of sleep when I feel an all-too-familiar rolling sensation. Bolting upright, I panic, thinking it's an earthquake...then I realize I'm in Kansas, not Los Angeles, and it's probably just a mind-trick being played by my perpetually fried jet lag brain. The next morning, I walk into the large gymnasium for my workshop and thirty-five women yell simultaneously,

"DID YOU FEEL IT?"

It turns out, what I felt the night before, really *was* a rather large earthquake; the epicenter was in Oklahoma, but everyone in Manhattan, Kansas could feel it!

After a full day of workshops, I am in my hotel room preparing for the show with Maharet, my Missouri sponsor who'd arrived in Kansas that afternoon. Maharet is taking me back to Missouri after this event, for more workshops and another show the next weekend. Suddenly, there's another earthquake. This time, since I am wide-awake, I know it's real.

"You brought that with you from LA!", Maharet declares, as we leave for the show.

As I take the stage for my entrance, I spy something out of the corner of my eye, swirling around in the air. At first, I think it's my veil flying from my spins, until I notice many concerned audience members whispering to each other, pointing animatedly to the stage. I look up, and notice there is a large bat flying around the stage... *and he's upstaging me!* The show grinds to a halt while the bat is captured in a trashcan, and removed during intermission by helpful belly dance husbands. I accompany them outside to watch it's safe release; as they let it go, I realize that without the full wingspan, the bat is much smaller than I initially thought.

Back at the hotel, Maharet and I laugh about the earthquakes and the bat. We set our phones for 7:30 am, confirming to each other that the clocks are being turned back to Standard Time that night. On the dot at 6:30am, her phone rings loudly. She mumbles that we still have another hour, so we go back to sleep. At 7:30 both our phones go off and Maharet is surprised that hers rang twice. I wonder aloud if it's the time change, and check the clock on the bed stand, but it's not on.

"Our clock's broken", I announce sleepily, and try turning on the lamp, which also doesn't go on. The bathroom light isn't working, either.

"Is this your *Electrical Disturbance*?" Maharet asks.

Peering out into the hallway, all I see are the EXIT signs. Finally, my eyes make out two teenage girls in pajamas shambling down the hallway like zombies.

"Are the lights out in the whole hotel?" I inquired.

They answer yes, and I ask, " Do you know why?"

"No," shrugged one, "We just accepted it."

With that, they shuffle off into the darkness.

I feel my way through packing my class materials like Helen Keller as Maharet gets us the last two cups of lukewarm coffee from the lobby. We arrive in class and luckily, the lights have been restored. Apparently, a huge apartment complex that was under construction has burned to the ground, causing a power outage in most of the city.

The next day, as we prepare to leave for Missouri, Maharet discovers she suddenly has no brakes in her car; it turns out there's a huge fluid leak. We buy a large container of break fluid, dreading the fact that we'll have to pull over every few miles on the long drive to Missouri to replenish the supply for safety's sake.

We join film director Steve Balderson for breakfast, and upon leaving his house, we all   hear a loud, odd sizzle and look up towards the noise, watching in horror as a poor little squirrel gets fried to death on the electrical lines above us. He hangs limp, his tail sadly blowing in the wind.

Steve has set us up with his friend Kathleen, who is a psychic healer, so her office is our next stop. The healings take about an hour each. I go first, and when I grant permission for Kathleen to "enter" me, I begin to feel jolts of electricity coursing through my body, from my left shoulder, across to the right one, pulsing down my leg into the right foot, and then going up the left side in the same way. This continues until I am literally bouncing on the table like a rag doll, my teeth chattering. I feel like The Monster just before Dr. Frankenstein screams, "It's alive.... *alive*!"

52

Maharet tells me I look ten years younger, though I am so wobbly I can barely walk. She has her healing, and emerges an hour later, announcing that she has given Kathleen one of her horses as a spirit guide. They make arrangements for Kathleen to pick it up before Maharet and I say our good byes and hit the road. The moment we get on the highway, it begins pouring rain. A few exits later, it becomes worse, the rain is torrential, it's going *sideways*. After about an hour, it's so bad that we pull over for coffee, hoping for the storm to pass. It doesn't, so we decide to drive again.

As Maharet puts the key in the ignition, the burglar alarm goes off. It's a relentless, rhythmic honking of the car's horn. She removes the key, and somehow, the alarm continues to wail. After five full minutes of chaos, Maharet calls her husband, and yells above the noise, trying to get him to figure out what's wrong. He tells her the alarm had been disconnected, and can't figure it out on the phone, so we sit in the car until a middle aged, mustachioed trucker tries to come to our aid. He can't figure out what's wrong, either. Finally, the noise dies down and we take off, thinking the car alarm's battery has died. No such luck: as we push forward through the driving rain, every time Maharet even taps the breaks, the alarm sounds wildly. We steel ourselves to the din, turn up the radio and scream to each other over the music, gossiping and telling stories.

An hour later, approaching Kansas City, it's now completely dark. The rain hasn't let up one iota... *and neither has the alarm*! It's rush hour, and the beltway around the city is crowded. Since the weather is so bad and the highway is backed up with cars, Maharet is on the brakes constantly, and the horn is sounding non-stop. Truckers are flipping us off, people are flashing their lights –as well as really dirty looks- at us.

An hour after that, we're driving through the hilly, unlit roads of rural Missouri. It's so dark and deserted, I almost expect a UFO to appear right above us...but the sound of the alarm, which is still going off, probably prevents our abduction.

Somehow, we make it home. Maharet's husband Bill comes to the door before the car is even parked, saying he heard us approaching from very far away. Once in the house, Maharet heads directly to the liquor cabinet, pulling out a two glasses and a bottle of Wild Turkey American Honey, which we down immediately before staggering into bed.

The next day, Bill starts the car, and the alarm seems to have magically fixed itself- there is absolutely *nothing* wrong with it.

53

HAPPY NEW YEAR FROM BEYOND

In 1999, during the days leading up to The New Millennium, like many people, I began reflecting on life: historical events I had witnessed, personal goals that I had achieved and the things I still wanted to accomplish. But what seemed to really dominate my thoughts were the many significant relationships I had with family and friends. I was blessed with so much love, nurture and support. I thought of the many special people who were there for me not matter what... friends and relatives who shared their lives with me, gave me affection, support and influenced my creative and artistic endeavors. One of these special individuals was my friend and belly dance mentor, the late Zein Abdul Al Malik.

Zein was a male dancer of prodigious talent. Well over six feet tall and lanky, he had piercing green eyes and performed draped in billowing genie pants and luxurious folkloric garb, wrapped in antique Egyptian Assuit, a traditional mesh fabric that has small strips of silver hammered into it to form designs. Zein looked imposing and exotic balancing a huge brass tray with a full tea set and candles upon his regal head. He started his career in the San Francisco Bay Area in the mid Seventies, dancing with one of the mothers of contemporary belly dance, Jamilla Salimpour. He went on to live in Morocco and Saudi Arabia, where he resided in one of the royal palaces, thanks to his Saudi prince lover. Zein lived and breathed Oriental Dance, performing, teaching and doing research.

After we met in 1990, he took me under his wing- *me, a beginning baby belly dancer with barely any skills-* but somehow he saw my potential and nurtured me. Zein would have me over to his apartment- a wonderful, mysterious enclave of inlaid North African furniture, luxurious plants and relics from the Middle East.

He'd make fresh mint tea in a silver Moroccan teapot and we'd spend hours together while he showed me steps and technique, discussed belly dance traditions, and watched vintage clips that he'd taped from the television in Saudi Arabia, featuring 1940's and '50's "Golden Age" Egyptian movies which starred famous dancers like Naima Akef, Samia Gamal, and Tahiya Carioca. Zein also helped me select costumes, heartily encouraged my dancing, and got me my very first dance job at Hollywood's Moun Of Tunis Restaurant, where he worked. More than two decades later, whenever I am in Los Angeles, I still perform there.

Appropriate music for Middle Eastern dance was hard to find in America back in those days, and Zein made me many Arabic mix tapes- remember, there were no CD's back then- with the cassettes featuring everything from classic live Om Kalthoum performances to the latest in Egyptian pop and Algerian Rai music. Every cassette Zein made me also had a special cover that he thoughtfully put together by hand. Some featured Middle Eastern clip art others photocopy of vintage Turkish cigarette boxes and pictures of famous belly dancers like Nagwa Fouad and Soheir Zaki.

Tragically, Zein died about five years after I met him. By that time, because of his encouragement, we were not only close friends but gigging together regularly. I was absolutely *devastated*. I remember speaking-or rather blubbering through a speech- at his memorial, my face wet with flowing tears, but I don't remember a thing I said.

After his death, I thought of him often, so many things reminded me of him. At gigs whenever I felt pre-show jitters, I would think of the way he used to calm my nerves through his twisted humor right before we both went on. Wrapped in a turban and wearing a brocade *galibiya*, shimmying to warm up, with an ever-present Marlboro in his mouth, Zein would sense my anxiety, catch my eye, make an exaggerated coquettish gesture then and whisper in a feminine falsetto,

"How's my hair?"

Somehow, our private joke never got old, and always made me laugh. Whenever he did that, I had a great show, entering the stage with a huge grin on my face. Even though Zein has been departed for years, I *always* think of him just before I go on.

So...fast forward to New Year's Eve 1999, at five minutes of midnight. Of *course* I was at a belly dance gig, in a dressing room, wearing a brand new costume- *my first costume for the New Millennium*.

The dancer I was working with that evening asked what music I was planning to perform to for my first dance set of the century.

"I don't know, " I said, pawing through my CD binder, "I'm so *sick* of all my music!"

My gig bag was full of the usual belly dance accoutrements: stray finger cymbals, perfume, hair accessories, mis-matched sequin armbands, loose aspirin tablets, safety pins.

56

Suddenly, something fell into my hands, a small plastic case. Though my suitcase was always chaotic, there was a method to my madness, and it was always re-packed before every show. The little plastic box was an unfamiliar object that I didn't remember packing that night. Recognizing what it was in the dim dressing room lighting by the feel of it, I wondered how it got there.

"Hey, no way, there's a *cassette* in my dance bag!" I cried, kind of amazed.

"*You still use cassettes?*" the other dancer asked incredulously.

"Well, no, not for years", I answered, dumbfounded,

"I have no idea what it's doing in here!"

"Well, maybe we can dance to it," she said, "What is it?"

I glanced at the clock- it was now one minute before midnight. Thinking we'd better figure our music out, I turned the mystery cassette case over in my hands. The cover featured a black and white drawing of a 1920's flapper lounging in a champagne glass.

In hand-lettered Art Deco font, it read:

"HAPPY NEW YEAR! LOVE, ZEIN"

As the clock struck midnight and the new century began, I got chills.

EVERYTHING'S COMING UP ROSES

I was singing "Auld Lang Syne" at the top of my lungs along with the car radio as I sped down the deserted 210 Freeway in the pre-dawn hours, heading towards Pasadena. A mere couple of hours ago, it had been New Year's Eve 1996. I had flown in from the East Coast earlier that day, and spent the evening- including the customary midnight count-down complete with a champagne toast- belly dancing my ass off at my regular gig, Moun Of Tunis Restaurant in Hollywood. In the couple of hours it had been 1997, I had just completed a show at a private party in West LA and now I was dead tired but I was excited- *I was going to dance in the 108th Tournament Of Roses Parade!*

The belly dance troupe I belonged to, Flowers Of The Desert Arabian Dance Company was performing as part of a float whose theme was world peace, ethnic diversity and cultural unity. The float's sponsors had envisioned kind of a rolling, posey and plant-studded version of Disneyland's "It's A Small World", but instead of the puppets and dolls that many floats feature, the dancers were going to be real people.

The Rose Parade is annually seen on television by more than 32 million viewers world-wide, and though I had always enjoyed laying around with champagne hangover, watching the parade and it's riot of colorful flowers, baton-twirlers and innovative, clever displays, I had never experienced it live- let alone been a part of it! Every float in the parade portrays it's own theme, and they're custom constructed weeks in advance of the event, parked in huge refrigerated warehouses while hundreds of volunteers painstakingly glue on flower petals, leaves, ferns, seeds and other natural bits of flora. Since I suffer from hay fever, I had taken the precaution of fortifying myself with Benedryl, so I wouldn't be sneezing and wheezing my way down the long parade route. I finally arrived in the designated parking area for the parade performers in the pitch black of the wee hours. Of course, in the pandemonium, it took me ages to find a parking space, and even longer for me to find the rest of my dance troupe and the float we were affiliated with!

It was utter chaos: in the gathering masses, I pushed past police barricades, entire families who had been camped out on the street for days to get a good spot on the parade route, television cameras and news crews doing pre-event coverage, staggering drunks, fire trucks, ambulances and tourists with huge mobile homes who had come to watch the big game, which kicked off directly following the parade.

The throngs of other parade participants probably numbered in the thousands. There were high school marching bands packed so closely that their tubas and trombones were clanking together; cheerleading squads from across the nation were practicing their moves next to equestrian groups with trick-riders dressed as cowboys and caballeros, and of course, The Budweiser Clydesdales, whose extensive, semi-truck-sized transportation trailers practically formed their own village.

The Clydesdales and other horses were all beautiful, and their riders looked festive, but their presence, along with the mounted police, also meant that there was a *ton* of horse shit on the street, so I had to pick my way very carefully in the dark to make sure I wouldn't get any on my Hermes sandals or the hem of my voluminous skirts.

Trying to locate the other Flowers Of The Desert, I encountered acrobatic troupes, soap opera stars, vintage car clubs with elderly members dressed as 1950's teenagers, NASA astronauts, military regiments, Ballet Folklorico dancers, Victorian Christmas carolers, and what seemed like zillions of Disney cartoon characters whose plush costumes and over-sized fake heads I used to think of as claustrophobic, but now envied cause I was so damn chilly in my own skimpy belly dance costume. Finally, I found my girls, resplendent in a glittering array of ethnic dance apparel, from Saudi *thobes* to silk pantaloons and *Ghawazee* dresses. They were clustered in a tight circle, huddled together for warmth. It was so cold I could see their breath as they greeted me through chattering teeth.

There are strict rules for Rose Parade participants. One of them is that since there is nowhere to change, you must arrive in full costume. No performer is allowed to bring *anything* with them on a float: no food, water bottles, purses, or even jackets. Hence, the goose bumps on all the participants who were dressed scantily, like the poor majorettes and us belly dancers. My house key and a couple of bucks were concealed in the bra of my costume. But while the other Flowers were clutching their chiffon veils around them in an unsuccessful attempt to retain body heat, I'd had the foresight to wear a raggedy old hoodie sweatshirt for pre-parade protection. I figured I would ditch it at the very last moment before the parade started at 7:00am. Unfortunately, that was still a couple of hours away. Even in my hoodie, it was freezing! Not only that, I was becoming ravenous, and sure I wouldn't last throughout the long morning without a bite to eat. Deciding it was time to take action, I asked a friendly- looking parade official if there was anywhere to get warm, and he directed me to a Red Cross station set up specially to serve the parade performers.

"You can't miss it," he said, looking me up and down and then snapping a picture of me with a disposable camera,

"It's right around the corner, a big mobile home- you can get all toasty in there. They have coffee and snacks for everyone in the parade."

I asked the other gals if they wanted to go with me but they were concerned we'd miss our cue for the parade's line-up if we left. For me, the bone-chilling dampness and the antihistamines I had taken, combined with my jet-lag, multiple-gig fatigue and growling stomach was taking a toll, and I informed them I was going to look for snacks and coffee and would bring some back. Heading off in the direction the parade official pointed me in I wandered down a residential street as dawn broke, in search of warmth, caffeine and hopefully a sandwich. I was almost crying with relief as I spotted the large trailer, right where the guy said it would be.

I trudged up the rickety, portable aluminum stairs of the mobile home, gathering my sequined skirts so I wouldn't trip. As I stepped into the cozy trailer, I closed my eyes in contentment as I felt the warmth envelop me. *I couldn't believe that the place wasn't packed full!* Happily, I smelled fresh coffee. I grabbed an apple off the counter and bit into lustily it before making my skirt-swishing, coin-jingling way to the bathroom to check my make-up in the tiny, fluorescent-lit space. Even though it had been on all night, my lipstick was intact, and my whole face was so bright and glittery that I was satisfied everyone, even in nosebleed seats of the bleacher stands would be able to see how glamorous and exotic I was.

Someone had thoughtfully left some perfume out on the sink counter, so I helped myself to that, too, splashing it on generously. As I stepped out of the tiny powder room, holding my half-eaten apple, the door slammed, almost hitting a gentile-looking older lady in a Christmas sweater.

"Oops! I'm so sorry!" I called out as I plopped down onto a couch, grabbing a donut and making myself at home.

"Do you guys have some coffee for me?"

My request was greeted with silence, but I didn't care since it was so warm in there and I was busy finishing up my apple and starting in on a donut.

"May I have some coffee, *please*?" I repeated.

After a long pause, a man's voice asked solicitously,

"Sure, how do you take it?"

As I looked up to answer him, suddenly things came into focus. Neither the man or the woman in the Christmas sweater were wearing any sort of Red Cross name tag or identification... in fact, there was *nothing* in the entire trailer at all that was even remotely connected to The American Red Cross: no posters, no literature, no visible signage.

There was a tiny, static-ridden portable TV showing pre-parade coverage, framed family photos on the walls, and some pillows and a Mexican blanket covering another couch, suggesting it had been very recently used as a bed. A large Golden Retriever with a holiday-themed bandanna around it's neck was snoozing on the couch near where I had sat down, and a half-completed knitting project lay on the table. The man was gray-haired and kindly looking, wearing a football jersey and he had his arm around the lady in the Christmas sweater. I gulped, realizing that I had stepped into a *private motor home!*

Then it came to me that I must've looked like an escapee from a mental hospital. I was a blatant, un-abashed trespasser with a sense of grandiose entitlement, bleary in my Benedryl haze. My face was caked with garish stage make up. I was a lunatic clad in a revealing belly dance costume topped by a dirty, ripped-up gray sweatshirt that even a refugee would be ashamed to wear. Not only that, I was holding the core of the recently devoured stolen apple in my hand and I reeked of the lady's perfume.

"Oh my God, I'm *so sorry!*" I spluttered, my face turning crimson with embarrassment.

The couple tried to keep straight faces- apparently, they had understood *exactly* what was going on the moment I crashed into their trailer, and were waiting to see how long it would take me to catch on.

"The Red Cross trailer is *next door*," the man said, deadpan,

"But you can still have some coffee...and we promise not to tell anyone what you did if you take a picture with us!"

At that, we all burst into laughter, even though mine was pretty sheepish. Turned out they were formerly from Pasadena, but now lived in Idaho.

They were in town for a few days to visit friends, see the game and watch the parade. They said that they'd made the pilgrimage to Pasadena every year for the past decade. Luckily, they were thrilled to see a glamorous- though very disoriented and sleep-deprived parade performer- come crashing into their world. We posed for a few photos, and then amidst more laughter, I left to find my sister dancers, who wondered aloud where I'd been for so long.

"Why didn't you come to the Red Cross trailer?" they squealed.

"It was *awesome*, everyone was so nice!"

I started to tell them, but we got rounded up in the appearance order for the floats along with all the other performers, because the parade was about to begin.

At 7:00am, The Stealth Bomber flew over downtown Pasadena, creating an earth-shaking sonic boom, which kicked off the festivities that year. As the floats revved their motors and the procession started, we rounded the first bend on the route, and there was literally a wall of television cameras. The sound of the crowds in the stands and on the streets was beyond deafening. The bands were all playing different songs at the same time; spectators were screaming and yelling and there was incessant bleating from those plastic parade horns that vendors sell to kids on the streets during events such as this.

After about forty minutes, my hip sockets felt like they were ground to dust and my feet began throbbing from the constant dancing. My face hurt from non-stop smiling and both my arms were sore from waving. People cut out of the crowds, zipping from the sidewalk to the floats, offering Dixie cups full of water for the all the performers.

Halfway through the route, parade spectators who were obviously locals held up large, hand-lettered signs with slogans reading:

ONLY 1.5 MILES TO GO!   THE END IS NEAR!

HANG IN THERE!

By the end of the parade route, I was completely exhausted; spent, utterly finished. I was so tired I didn't even want to get a VIP close-up look at any of the other floats; I just wanted to get home and go to sleep. But in spite of everything, I was still grinning ear-to-ear and laughing to myself, because I couldn't possibly think of a better way to ring in the New Year!

THE KING AND I

The security line at Dallas-Fort Worth Airport was ridiculously long, and the TSA officials seemed to be ultra-paranoid, checking and re-checking toddler's bottles, tearing apart well-packed quart baggies, patting down old ladies, and treating everyone in the queue with suspicion. I was sweating bullets for no other reason than because I was already insanely late for my plane to Los Angeles.

During the weekend belly dance show I'd performed on in Grapevine, Texas, I'd been hanging out my new friend Tamra Henna, a fantastic local belly dancer whom I'd recently dubbed "Tex". Tex and I had gotten along like gangbusters, so well that she'd offered to drive me to the airport. Over lunch at a taco stand, we discussed everything from vintage Egyptian cinema and our favorite Arabic songs to stage make-up and the craziest, weirdest gigs we'd both been hired for. Since it seemed like I had plenty of time until my flight, and we were both hopelessly addicted to glitter in general and belly dance costumes in particular, we mutually made the executive decision to stop at Little Egypt Imports.

"You will *not* believe this place!" Tex promised, as she barreled down the highway,

"You're totally gonna lose it when you see all the stuff they have!"

She suddenly swerved her car into a driveway and parked in front of a huge building with rusted corrugated metal siding.

"Here we are!" she exclaimed triumphantly, while I wondered what in the hell this giant airplane hangar could possibly have to do with belly dancing.

As we stepped through the door, I realized that the whole place was Little Egypt Imports. It was as though the entire Valley of the Kings had been teleported into this colossal Quonset hut and then dropped directly onto Texan soil. One room was full of gleaming, enormous pieces of heavy, carved wooden furniture decorated with hieroglyphics and cartouches, gaily painted in a rainbow of colors, strewn hand-woven, tasseled brocade pillows. There were seven foot tall statues depicting Isis and Osirus, Horus, Hathor, Queen Hatshepsut and Bast; gold-leaf busts of Nefertiti, blue ceramic scarab and hippotamus paper weights, and an over-sized reproduction of King Tut's sarcophagus, which, when opened, revealed an interior decorated as sumptuously as it's outside shell. I was flabbergasted...I never even knew stuff like this existed outside of an actual museum!

Breathless with excitement, I tore over to the rooms that featured the belly dance costumes, and promptly immersed myself in the endless racks of rhinestone-embellished goodies. Tex and I each tried on countless costumes, sighing over the Egyptian finery, longingly fingering the hand-beaded details. In our frenzied process, we promptly lost our street clothes amidst knee-high piles of glittering chiffon hip-scarves, their coins jingling merrily as we trudged through them, looking for one of my shoes.

Finally done with the costumes, we eagerly asked about Isis Wings. Though now a belly dance staple, Isis Wings were hard to come by back then. They are glamorous, huge, pleated metallic chiffon wings with sticks concealed the ends to increase their span. At the beginning of the New Millennium almost no dancers had them unless they'd been custom made...but Little Egypt had *scads* of them, in every hue.

Seizing this magnificent opportunity and standing at the counter still minus my missing shoe, I negotiated a great price and selected a beautiful gold lame' set of wings for myself. They were packed up for me in a darling little custom carrying case, which resembled a long, blue vinyl tube with handles. Suddenly snapping back into reality and realizing what time it was, Tex and I made a mad dash for the car and then she drove like NASCAR champion to DFW airport.

Since I'd only brought a small suitcase to the belly dance event, I decided to check my bag and carry my coveted, fragile Isis Wings into the plane's cabin with me, rather than cramming them in along with my costumes. Tex reassured me that I was making the right decision- *the wings were simply too rare and delicate to relegate to a checked bag!* We quickly said our good byes at the loading zone curb and I made a mad dash for my gate after checking my bag.

So there I was in the TSA security line, tenderly cradling my newly purchased Isis wings, stressing about whether I'd actually be let onto the plane, which was scheduled to depart in about twenty minutes. The line was moving at a snail's pace, and I was still not through security. Finally, it was my turn. I lovingly slid my wings safely into a plastic bin and sent them on their way down the conveyor belt into the X-Ray machine. A seasoned traveler, I had removed any accessories that might have set off the metal detector and passed through easily. But the moment I thought I was free and clear, an obese female TSA agent began carelessly waving around my Isis wing carrying case, screaming in a nasal Plains twang that could only be described as The Trailer Trash Accent, yelling:

"WHO DIS BELONGS TO?"

As I stepped up to claim my precious package, she demanded an explanation as to what, exactly, it was. I realized immediately that I'd be much better off not mentioning *anything* about belly dancing, assuming she'd somehow equate an Egyptian dance accessory with Arab Terrorists. As the woman gave me the stink eye, looking at me with a mixture of contempt and distrust, I noticed the perspiration rings under her tightly fitting uniform...apparently she took her job very seriously. I also saw that she had an inordinate amount of dandruff, not to mention an IQ that was probably just *barely* in the double digits.

She repeated her question, blowing breath that reeked of Corn Nuts directly into my face,

"WHAT IS DIS?"

Keeping an even, cheerful tone, I said as nonchalantly as possible,

"Oh, I'm an *actress* from Los Angeles, and those are just... a set of big butterfly wings, I use them in a *play*, they're part of a *stage costume.*"

"WELL IT HAS RODS IN IT!" she huffed, "WHY THEM RODS IN THAAAYR?"

Beginning to seriously panic, with the seconds ticking away til my flight departed, I thought fast. What I needed was *damage control-* otherwise I was going to be spending the night on the floor in the airport!

"Why those aren't rods," I said as sweetly as I could muster,

"Those are just like...little, tiny, skinny balsa-wood sticks... you know, like for a *paper airplane*? Just little... Popsicle sticks! Those aren't rods... They're just pieces of craft-wood, light as a feather!"

My voice trailed away as she regarded me sternly, as though I was a seasoned Plutonium smuggler, or some crazy criminal who just happened to be plotting a skyjacking with a set of newly purchased Isis Wings.

"WHY DIN' YOU CHECK THIS?" she snarled, as though I was trying to bring an automatic weapon on board with me.

Breath, I kept repeating to myself... just breathe.... you can *do* this.

"Well, ma'am, it's just a very delicate stage costume," I said quite earnestly, "I was afraid to check them, because I thought they'd get ruined."

"AHMONNA HAFTA CALL A SUPERVISOR!" she bellowed, and immediately made an announcement on the loudspeaker.

More time went by as we both waited for the supervisor to show up. Finally, I saw him coming. A dyed-in-the-wool *Good Ole Boy*, he ambled up to the security line, his TSA uniform augmented with cowboy boots, a straw cowboy hat, and a fancy silver rodeo belt buckle. He was rolling a wooden toothpick around in his mouth.

"JES' WHASS GOIN' ON AROUN' HYAAAR?" he asked, hooking his thumbs into the rodeo belt, cocking his head to the side as he sized me up.

Immediately, I knew I had to play The Belly Dance Card. To someone like him, a true redneck, the mere words "belly dance" would probably get him all warm and fuzzy...or *hot 'n' bothered* as the case may be... probably bringing to mind fond memories of wet T-shirt contests and bachelor-party pole dances. Though usually annoying, the general public's misconception of Oriental Dance sometimes does, indeed, come in handy!

Standing straight up and thrusting my chest out so he had a direct sigh-line to my cleavage, I said in what I hoped was a tone of voice that sounded like I was a bona fide Reality Show Bimbo,

"Hi sir! I'm a *belly dancer!*"

He looked me up and down through narrow eyes, chewing contemplatively on his toothpick.

"A BELLY DANCUH, HUH?" he grunted.

"Oh yes I am!" I answered, batting my eyelashes and twirling my hair flirtatiously.

"WELP, SHE SAID YOU HAD SOME RODS IN THAAYR, MIND IF I TAKE A LOOK?"

"Oh no sir," I simpered, "Please go right ahead."

He un-zipped my case, and began palpating it, before pulling out yards...and yards...and even more yards of pleated, metallic fabric. Finally, he narrowed his eyes and addressed me, scratching under the brim of his cowboy hat.

"WHUD YEW SAYS THIS WAS AGIN?"

"It's a *stage costume*, sir!"

I wiggled a little to drive my point home before throwing a beaming grin in his direction. As he fingered the material thoughtfully, suddenly it looked like a light bulb went off in his head.

"HEY! I KNOW WHAT THISSY-HYAAR IS!" he smiled,

"THIS IS JES' LIKE ELVIS, INNIT IT?"

I didn't have the foggiest notion of what he meant by that comment, but eager to please him, and more than eager to *maybe actually make my plane*, I nodded enthusiastically. If The King was something that would get me on my flight, I'd be more than happy to accept the comparison.

"Yes! Why, yes it is just *exactly* like Elvis!" I agreed.

"OH," he grumbled to the female TSA agent,

"SHE AIN'T GONNA DO NUTHIN' WITH THIS! LET HER BE!"

With that, I grabbed my wings and ran like hell to my gate. I was the last passenger to board the flight. Puzzled by the entire thing and mulling the incident over in my head, it wasn't til our aircraft was over Arizona that I realized what that supervisor had thought my wings were: those Super Hero circle-shaped capelets that Elvis had worn over his jumpsuits, towards the end of his career, when he was in his Fat Phase.

Now, years later, every time I don a pair of Isis Wings before a performance, I breathe a silent prayer of thanks to The King.

HEARTBREAK HOTEL

Valentine's Day... just the thought of it makes me queasy. I've had so many weird and hellish Valentine's Days, I often entertain the fantasy of going into hibernation on February 13th and then just popping out emotionally unscathed in the wee hours of February 15th to shoot a lingering sidelong glance at my shadow. Come to think of it, my shadow has probably been the most stable and enduring relationship I've ever had!

Don't get me wrong- I've actually been very lucky in love and love gettin' lucky, but in my regards to Valentine's Day itself-and my surviving it- it's a wonder I haven't been a recipient of the Purple Heart, for sheer bravery, valor and life-threatening battle wounds. In fact, the military-slogan-bearing T-shirts stretched across the buff chests of our country's off-duty armed forces can best sum up my personal Valentine's Day experiences:

I KNOW I'M GOING TO HEAVEN, CAUSE I'VE DONE MY TIME IN HELL!

Or better yet:

KILL 'EM ALL...LET GOD SORT IT OUT!

I remember one Valentine's Day when the only item in my mailbox that even remotely resembled a heart was a red notice from a utility company. As if that wasn't bad enough, my evening was packed with shows that only served to rub my "single" status in my face: every damn place I danced was so full of cooing couples I felt like I was performing on Noah's Ark!

Then there was the February 14 back in the early 1980's... the date I picked, as a hopeless twenty-year-old romantic, to be My Wedding Day. In our sole nod to tradition, my groom and I arrived separately (and not *too* hung over) at the hall where our ceremony, which had been booked for the better part of a year, was to be held.

I was a vision in an ivory Fifties strapless organza gown, with an over-lay of French lace embroidered with seed pearls. My hair, bleached White Minx, was in a fetching Monroe bob, and under my Goodwill steal of a Juliet veil, I sported my customary Revlon Cherries In The Snow lipstick. As I daintily stepped out of the car gathering my train, I was astounded to see dozens of buckets of carnations which had been dyed an uproarious shade of baby blue.

As I wondered who'd Dumpster-dived the LA Flower District in honor of my wedding, I spotted legions of Low Riders, uniformly bedecked in powder blue Polyester double-knit tuxes. Tattooed jailhouse tears and pompadours covered by homeboy hairnets abounded. The four hundred or so bridesmaids were a symphony in ruffled dresses so tight and shiny they looked like they were auditioning to be the Shark's molls in a special baby blue colorized version of Westside Story. Just as I was starting to realize that this was not the result of my hangover or an LSD flashback and that Mr. Colorization himself, Ted Turner hadn't been invited, the Unitarian priest who was presiding over my ceremony came rushing out to explain to my groom and I -*and three quarters of East LA*- that the hall had been accidentally double booked.

Tension ran high for a moment, but at the minister's gentle suggestion we finally decided that a coin-toss was in order. While disgruntled guests from both camps fumbled for quarters, I heard The Best Man whisper to my groom that he had a full tank of gas, a fifth of Scotch, two hundred bucks... and that The Border was only three hours away. Before my betrothed had a chance to answer, someone pulled out a coin, we won the flip, and had our ceremony first, amongst the blinding neon blue riot of dyed flowers. Speaking of *first*, I should've taken the scheduling snafu as an omen- that turned out to be just My First Wedding. If there are any photos that somehow survived being cut-up or burned, I can assure you they are predominantly baby blue.

Many years later, I foolishly accepted a Valentine's Day date with Art Boy, to his first major gallery opening. Why I did it, I'll never know; I was in the throws of an obsessive crush on my best friend, the sexually ambiguous Collegiate Art Department Head, whom Art Boy and I had met in happier times at The Blacklite, an infamous Hollywood dive bar, frequented by a garish parade of luridly made-up trannie hookers.

And there was another little glitch: Art Boy and I had been... just a teensy bit broken up -*oh, excuse me, I really meant to say totally hostile and incommunicado*- for months.

But hearing Art Boy's cajoling, purring voice, I magically seemed to forget all of that... as well as the fact that when Art Boy and I had originally embarked upon our passionate and *certifiably insane* affair three years previously-also coincidentally on February 14th - it had resulted in the spectacularly gut-wrenching dissolution of My Second Marriage. But Art Boy poured it on shamelessly. He really missed me, he was just *dying* to see me belly dance again! I caved.

So I went to Art Boy's opening, dressed for sin in a skin-tight black velvet cat suit and sky-high red platforms, glittering sequined hearts scattered throughout my ass-length, teased-up, mid 1960's Jacqueline Susann hair do. Art Boy was there, of course...*but I hadn't anticipated the bosomy redhead that was hanging all over him!*

Realizing I'd been used for a free performance, I bit the bullet and decided to dance anyway, seeing as how I was already there and it was so crowded, there'd be lots of potential tips. In my frazzled state, I started downing multiple plastic cups of the cheap swill that was barely passing for Merlot. I was starting my fifth drink when the disinterested gallery owner hustled me to a filthy, closet-sized bathroom, the only place in the gallery where I could change into my costume, since he wouldn't allow me to use his office.

I didn't realize that the toilet had been over-flowing until my gig bag had been sitting on the floor for quite some time... *because there was no light.* Foul mouthed drunks-people drunker than even I was, if that was *possible*-banged on the door as I changed into costume.

While I performed, the hem of my costume got drenched in the puddles of beer that had formed on the cement floor, and someone burned a hole in my veil with a cigarette. When I finished my show, Art Boy was macking ardently on the new gal. Instantly, drinks and insults were flung from both sides. My recollection is fuzzy, but I do believe I was the one that started it.

My oldest, most-trusted friend Bobby, who was visiting from Memphis, Tennessee, quickly escorted me out of the melee like the Gallant Southern Gentleman he always has been. Somehow, we wound up at The Blacklite. Collegiate Art Department Head was already there, much to my delight. Much to my dismay, he was there with a date. By the end of the night, I was infatuated with The Date, who looked like a cross between a gorgeous '70's glam rock fag and 6' 6" Hitler Youth, with the longest, blackest eyelashes I had ever seen- *and they were real!*

When the din of the jukebox died down, I detected a Euro Accent. I was madly drunk and melting from lust...and apparently, he was too. That Valentine's Day, we began or affair- and also a five year long merry-go-round of love, lies, sex, heartbreak, stalking, drug abuse, violence, and psychological torture between Department Head, Tomorrow Belongs To Him and lil' ole me. You name it, we experienced it. It was a Love Triangle Of Bermudic proportions.

Thank god, all that Valentine's Day insanity ended in the late 1990's.

I'd like to say I've *learned* from my experiences... but I know better. I seem to be feeling a little drowsy ...wake me up when it's over, will you?

THE MINX

In the late Seventies, The Palomino was *the* nerve center of country music in Los Angeles. The famed San Fernando Valley roadhouse had hosted Johnny Cash, Tammy Wynette, Jerry Lee Lewis and, like, and every other country star whose name meant *anything*. "The Pal", as regulars affectionately called it, might as well have been the West Coast wing of The Grand Ole Opry or Tootsie's Orchid Lounge, that's *jes' how country* it was. The air was so thick with a haze of cigarette smoke and clouds of cheap perfume smoke that it seemed like a gardenia-scented bomb had recently gone off. It was the type of place where the patrons really *did* sit at the bar drinkin' doubles and feelin' single.

The cocktail waitresses, all genuine Honky Tonk Angels and Buckle Bunnies who'd moved to LA from places like Bakersfield, Needles, and Lone Pine had aspirations of being the next Crystal Gayle. Their faces were uniformly hard-lined and overly made-up, and instead of Farrah-do's, they had big Nashville hair, teased and sprayed. Stealthy and discreet, with the finesse of thieves, they'd sidle up to tables on the pretense of clearing empty glasses while surreptitiously slipping their demo cassettes into the suit pockets of their Music Biz clientele.

I frequented The Pal but never really fit in, even though my boyfriend was the lead singer of the hugely popular neo-rockabilly group, Levi & The Rockats. Whenever I was there, it always felt like I was on a Black Ops mission, or as though I doing anthropological research. I was a stranger in a strange land- a clandestine punk rock refugee living a make-believe life, trying to pass as an urban cowgirl. In reality, even attired in my vintage 1950's Western wear, I was only fooling *myself.* With my bleached white, greased Elvis pomp and chipped metallic blue nail polish, I stuck out like a sore thumb amidst all the embroidered Nudie's rodeo duds and the tight Spandex, Tanya Tucker-iffic jumpsuits.

At least had company-I was usually with my all-time favorite partner in crime, The Minx. Not only was her guy the drummer in my boyfriend's band, The Minx shared my secret punk rock past. In her rockabilly phase, she looked like a miniature Italian movie star, circa 1959. But I knew better: it wasn't *always* that way.

The Minx swears I was the first punk rocker she'd ever met; that I changed her life. We'd first bumped into each other two years previously in 1976, at Granny Takes A Trip. The trendy, world-famous glitter-rock-gone-punk boutique had become famous on King's Road in

London, clothing everyone from Marc Bolan of T-Rex to The Sweet and Roxy Music. They had had just opened an offshoot store on Sunset Strip. Teenagers on leave from Suburbia, The Minx and I arrived there at the same time, both trying to sell T-shirts we'd made. Mine had dirty words stenciled in spray paint all over; hers had two zippers down the front which, when opened, would reveal the breasts. Initially, I looked upon her as my competition, but her lurid blue eye shadow, breathy voice and tiny hands immediately enchanted me.

Dainty and adorable, The Minx was- and still is- one of those girls who'll never look like a woman. With unusually large doe-eyes, a perfect tiny nose and close-cropped hair, she's the ultimate gamine. If you dressed her in a toga and put a wreath of flowers in her hair, or maybe added a set of gossamer wings, she could be reclining in a Maxfield Parish print. Compared to her stature, her personality is over-the-top; she's smart, brash and vibrant, more like an idealized Japanimation character than a *real person*. She was fun in big, fat primary-colored Fisher-Price letters; letters with googly eyes and little cartoon smiles. Fun like a tawdry carnival sideshow, fun like an old-time whorehouse, it's hallways filled with drunken conventioneers in boxer shorts and Fez hats. Fun like a dimly lit back-stage of a run-down cabaret in Weimar Republic Berlin. The Minx was always up for *anything*.

We became fast friends, seeing each other regularly at The Whisky A Go-Go for Ramones and Blondie shows, at The Masque for Germs gigs, and at many a drunken party at The Canterbury Arms, a run-down apartment building on Cherokee, just off Hollywood Boulevard. Many punks took up residence there, because the place was cheap… they rented to anybody, it was full of junkies and hookers, the manager was running scams with the landlord, and probably running drugs. The elevators were covered graffiti; constantly out of service. Rigs and beer cans were discarded on the shredded carpet in the hallways, which probably hadn't been replaced since the McCarthy era. The apartments themselves were great- or had once been. Big "starlet" singles from Hollywood's Golden Age, they all had built-in vanities and Murphy Beds.

There was typically a lot of Mickey's Big Mouth beer involved in the Canterbury shindigs. The stereo would be blasting latest The Clash or Adverts import 45 while people who were too young to drink legally locked themselves in the bathroom to do drugs. The walls in the Canterbury's kitchenettes were splattered from food-fights with day- old Top Ramen or Kraft Macaroni and Cheese; people were always passed

76

out on ratty sofas salvaged from the trash. Inevitably, a lot of drunken pogo dancing took place, and usually, a Murphy bed would come loose from it's hinges and slam off the wall and onto some hapless kid's head.

None of us had jobs, because you couldn't get hired if you had pink- or even dyed black hair. Our clothes came from dumpster-diving Salvation Army donation boxes, and we were always on the guest list for shows. As long as you had enough cash for cigarettes and beer, you were dandy. Nobody wanted a regular job, anyway. It would interfere with our parties.

We were wanna-be musicians who were also painters, photographers, performance artists, clothing designers, writers, dancers, actors and smart -though disenfranchised- suburban teenagers. There was also a bunch of older, off-the-wall types, refugees from the Midwest and New York, ex-hippies from Haight Ashbury, ex-Beats from North Beach and Greenwich Village, and former Superstars from Andy Warhol's Factory. Lots of us had come from the glitter rock scene, and so were comfortable with multiple partners and bisexuality. There were openly gay folks, but also those who were simply into experimentation, people who didn't really believe in *labels* or conventional lives. For a while, at the Canterbury, there was even a frisky, all-female club or gang (a la West Side Story) called the Piranhas. They were rumored to be a bunch of dykes, but were more like raunchy party girls, out for a good time and outrageous fun... and sex with anyone cute who presented themselves. All of us were infinitely unemployable, and we had to do *something* with our time, so we drank a lot, had tons of casual sex, formed bands, made Xeroxed fanzines, and drank and fucked some more.

Everything trendy in New York or especiall London had a huge influence on us, so when English punks started getting into Teddy Boy culture, listening to American roots music, wearing drape coats, suede Brothel Creeper shoes and voluminous poodle skirts, we all followed suit. It was only a matter of time until it was *de rigueur* to have a rockabilly paramour.

Always a step ahead of the crowd, The Minx and I swooped in and got the pick of the litter before any other punkettes got hip to the scene. Our boyfriends had migrated from London, via New York's Lower East Side, and were in the hottest- and at that point, *only* rockabilly band to hit the US, making all the girls in the audience swoon the way the chicks did in those ancient newsreels about "The Devil's Music".

It was a novelty to stand at the mouth of the stage and see handsome guys in suits and string ties crooning love songs. Much better that standing safely away from a roiling mosh pit full of boozed-up jocks slam dancing, or watching pasty-skinned, pimply guys covered in spit and beer screaming out one-chord songs about war and The Government ... *with fake English accents*. Rockabilly was *sexy*. It was about being horny, not being on The Dole.   Punk chicks by the dozen were abandoning their Converse high tops in favor of saddle shoes, trading in their Dead Kennedys T-shirts for bullet bras and tight cashmere sweaters, all to catch the eye of these cool hepcats.

My Cockney boyfriend Levi was a bona fide English Ted, and Dean, his drummer, whom The Minx was seeing, originally hailed from Kentucky, giving him even more rockabilly cred. He had a bleached blonde pompadour and a sleepy, Eddie Cochran smile. *Our* boys were in the band that was the toast of the town. We were madly in love with them, and the envy of every girl who hadn't already been growing her spiky hair out long enough to make a ponytail.

So there The Minx and I were at The Pal, already tipsy and excited because our hepcat beaux were opening for Ray Campi And The Rockabilly Rebels. Stand-up bassist Ray Campi was a living legend, a Texan who'd been at it since the early Fifties. His singer, Colin Winski, was tall and loose-hipped, with big sideburns and a cool yelping wail. Jerry Sikorski, the lead guitarist, looked like a cross between slightly wall-eyed, blond teddy bear and blank-faced Barney Rubble in the Flintstones... but he could do back-flips and summersaults with his axe strapped on, not missing a note. Our guys were duly impressed.

Of course there was an after-party, and The Minx and I steeled ourselves for the inevitable: hours of the guys spinning rare 45's and one-upmanship over who knew more facts about the obscure one-hit-wonders who were probably fat, old, John Deere cap-wearin' rednecks pumping gas in rural Arkansas by now. But, dutiful girlfriends that we were, we tagged along anyway.

The party was at Jerry Sikorski's place, a neatly kept Post WWII ranch house in the depths of San Fernando Valley tract-house suburbia... *where he still lived with his parents*. They happened to be gone for the weekend, he said enthusiastically, so it would be possible for the guys to *jam* together. The Minx and I could barely help rolling our eyes. These post-gig after parties had become a monotonous routine for our punkette souls, even though we wanted to be "good" girlfriends. It was hard to

tell what was a worse fate: standing around listening to the fraternity of drunken Sun Records wannabees warbling out Gene Vincent hits, or sitting there unable to get a word in edgewise while they played the entire collected works of Bill Haley and The Comets- or their offshoot band The Jodimars- on scratchy 78's, while everyone argued passionately about the bass-line.

The Sikorski house was comfy, homey and cluttered. Hand-crocheted Afghans draped the couch; a pile of *Family Circle*s was stacked neatly on the oversized television set. The super-sized fridge was full of beer, and things brightened up considerably when Colin passed a joint around while everyone plugged in mics and amps.

Bored already, I wandered through the house, impressed by the rampant normalcy, so *inviting* after staying at series of punk crash pads where the main source of nutrition was ketchup and mustard stolen from fast food joints. In the bathroom, I admired the ceramic angelfish figurines floating up the wall with morbid fascination. The Minx sauntered in, her crinolines swishing. I took a sip of the cocktail she offered, while re-applying my Revlon Cherries In The Snow lipstick. It was *the* perfect sex-kitten shade - the ultimate in '50s glamour. I had recently switched from using the punk lipstick of choice: Artmatic's Black Orchid, which was only forty-nine cents at Woolworth's. It was a deep, matte burgundy suitable for extras in *Night Of The Living Dead*, Puerto Rican drag queens or those endless Canterbury parties.

The Minx powdered her nose and feigned a yawn as I lit a cigarette. In the den, our boys were murdering The Johnny Burnette Trio's "Butterfingers." Together we inspected the master bedroom. The double bed had a golden vinyl headboard and a quilted yellow-ochre satin spread. A pair of bifocal reading glasses and a dog-eared *Reader's Digest* sat on the bedside table. I flopped onto the bed to adjust the seams of my hose, and The Minx sat down next to me.

Glancing down at my black fishnets, which would've been much more appropriate for *The Rocky Horror Show* or a spread in a late 1950's pulp detective magazine, suddenly everything became clear to me: all this rockabilly stuff was wearing thin. While the music was great, the teen idol stuff only went so far. Sure, our guys sang about back-seat, drive-in-movie sex and burnin' desires, but all they ever wanted to do in *real* life was have a couple of beers and boast about the rare records they'd found at swap meets and junk stores. The biggest drag was that they were constantly telling you not to mess up their hair, *even during sex*. Carefully coifed into brand new "Rebel Without A Cause" DA's and sculpted with Murray's Pomade, the rockabillies would spend hours hogging your bathroom mirror in displays of vanity that would've been off-putting even to Little Richard.

The punk guys, I recalled with new-found nostalgia, would let you dye their hair green, dripping Krazy Kolor all over their leathers and the bathroom floor. They'd allow you put make-up on them and would dress up in your underwear, dancing around to Donna Summer disco songs. They wanted to get wasted on hallucinogenics and have sex up against a dumpster in an alley...which might not have been the height of romance, but was *far* more exciting than listening to a bunch of guys in sharkskin suits jabbering away all night about Carl Perkins and Ersel Hickey.

The Minx and I, it occurred to me, were just as trapped as *real* 1950's women. It was only through obligation and loyalty that we found ourselves listening to endless sermons about the early days of Sun Records, dressed in our little Peter Pan-collared blouses, playing Suzi Homemaker, Donna Reed, and June Cleaver rolled into one. On the outside, we appeared to be Atomic Age arm-candy. Inside, we were both secretly pining away for some good old-fashioned debauchery. We didn't want to be prettyprettypretty Peggy Sue, or the virginal Deborah Padgett, Elvis' love interest in the movie "Loving You". What we *really* wanted was to be was Priscilla Presley after Elvis turned her into a hooker-looking version of "The Bride Of Frankenstein", with gobs of black eyeliner, wearing Bob Mackie gowns and drinking champagne while The King got wasted on Quaaludes and Dilaudid and shot out television sets in a Vegas penthouse suite. For weeks, our old punk rock selves had been coming back to re-claim our surrendered power and individuality. Slowly but surely, subversive black fishnet hose and garters started replacing our bobby sox. Ticking like teenage time bombs, our latent desire for something more decadent was coming to a head.

The Minx reached up to my face and gently wiped away a lipstick smudge. The next thing I knew, we were kissing.

It was tentative for a moment, but got increasingly wild and passionate. Coming up for air, we shared a brief, charged glance. I reached across her to the lamp on the nightstand and switched it off; we resumed kissing. I gently pushed her down onto the bed, and, as they say in romance novels, *she yielded to me*. We writhed around, breathless. Her lips were pillowy; I tasted our recently applied lipstick. She kissed in a languid, leisurely way, like a courtesan in a harem. She tasted like a divine mixture of cinnamon gum, cigarettes and vodka. Running her hands through my hair, her '50's crystal "grandma" necklace clattered against my teeth as I covered her neck with a flurry of love bites. My head was spinning from a combination of cocktails and lust.

Suddenly The Minx sat up, grabbed my face, and whispered urgently,

"I've fantasized about this for so long!"

Dumbfounded for a moment, almost expecting her to say she was joking, I stuttered,

"Me, too!"

"This has been a dream of mine," she said, as she rolled over on top of me and started undressing me slowly. I felt goose bumps covering my entire body as her hands slid up my thighs, lightly snapping the elastic of my vintage garter belt.

We fooled around for a long time, our purses, petticoats and pumps littering the floor. We squirmed our way through the guys doing Billy Lee Riley's "Flying Saucers Rock 'n' Roll", Jack Scott's "The Way I Walk", Warren Smith's "Ubangi Stomp" and – how utterly appropriate- Buddy Holly's nasty jump blues song about a cheating woman, "Annie's Been Working On The Midnight Shift".

It was not only completely thrilling to be with her- we were both feeling an illicit, delicious charge- having sex on a pristine bed, our friend's *parent's* bed, in a suburban ranch house, knowing that our unsuspecting boyfriends were in the very next room, completely oblivious to what we were doing. It was fabulous, wanton, and dirty as can be.

Finally, we both felt that we'd been AWOL for too long. I could hear my boyfriend and Colin belting out "Wake Up, Little Susie" by the Everly Brothers, so we took that as a call for reveille. Giggling and conspiratorial, we buckled up our push-up, bullet-shaped brassieres and hit the bathroom to comb our hair and fix our smudged lipstick.

The guys barely noticed us as we waltzed into the living room, asking like perky Eisenhower-era housewives if anyone wanted a cocktail. It was as though during our secret encounter we'd slid into a private *Twilight Zone* of teenage lust... and our boyfriends had no idea they'd provided the soundtrack!

THEM

The raven-haired, long-stemmed beauty sharing my bed stretched voluptuously as she rolled over to face me. She propped her chin up kittenishly on both hands as her dusky breasts strained at the sheer, diaphanous fabric of her Frederick's Of Hollywood push-up bra. Her eyes sought mine and her intimate, steady gaze never wavered as she asked me intently:

"Have you ever owned a vibrator?"

*   *   *

I guess I should really start at the beginning of this particular tale. The year was 1985. The raven-haired beauty was Laura Bennett, who was the   rhythm guitarist and sometime-bass player in my all-girl band the Screamin' Sirens, and also one of my roommates at Disgraceland.

Laura had come to my band- and to my infamous house- by way of Orange County.   My never-ending lust for beach-raised, Southern California skate-punk booty had drawn me away from my native Hollywood so I was spending a lot of time down in " The OC".

During the course of many inebriated nights at Huntington Beach punk rock hot-spots like Safari Sam's, Meadowlark Country Club and Spats, Laura and I were simultaneously engaged in a rousing game of musical beds with exactly the same   heartthrobs from the bands Tex And The Horseheads, TSOL, and the Vandals, as well as with world class skateboard champs straight out of the pages of *Thrasher*. Though it took us both a while to figure out what was happening, upon comparing notes later on, we realized that we were both oddly fascinated by this phenomenon. It got to the point where the romantic overlap between Laura and I became so ridiculous and French farce-like that my friend Keren Miller, aka Rag Girl, coined a new term for what Laura and I were doing: *Going Plaid.* But instead of staying romantic rivals, Laura and I decided we had to be friends...and we soon realized we had *a lot* more in common than the same boys.

Laura was in a Long Beach–based punky blues band called Hard As Nails Cheap As Dirt, a band whose decadent onstage shenanigans included having a poker table – *with a rousing card game going on around it*- set up right on the stage as they played.   This was a band whose big, crowd-pleasing hit song was called "The Back of Your Head Never Looked So Good".

Lead singer Smitty spent most of his time on stage writhing around on the floor, screaming unintelligible lyrics into the mic while desperately kicking at Laura's petticoats, trying to get a look up her dress. Smitty himself had picked out the band's name at random from a classified ad hawking VHS porn tapes in the back of Hustler magazine. The name fit the band- and Laura- perfectly.

Like me and my beloved Disgraceland roommate Iris Berry, rock and roll was Laura's life, and she also shared our ability to easily go along with any sort of insane adventure that presented itself, all while managing to remain innocently dewy-faced in spite of a love for Jack Daniels that would've put even David Lee Roth to shame.

Laura also had a predilection for a punk ingénue wardrobe staple that Iris and I referred to as *Binge Dresses*. A necessary part of our lives back then, Binge Dresses were very Ellie Mae Clampett On A Lost Weekend. They were cheery, lace-trimmed floral or gingham 1950's and '60's day shifts that were innocuous and cute, but more importantly *comfortable...* whether you were passed out on a strange sofa or spending endless hours on tour in a van with no air-conditioning. Binge Dresses, entirely against all odds over the course of a multi-day poly-substance abuse marathon, were like a special force field that made you looks somehow *presentable*, even when the police inevitably busted the party you were having. And no matter how wasted you were, if you had on a Binge Dress, it enabled you to retain an absolutely fresh and fuckable appearance. A good Binge Dress would remain spotless and wrinkle-free for days, no matter what you did: whether you jumped fully clothed into a swimming pool, rolled in puddles of spilled beer on the floor of a club, bled from cuts incurred while hopping a barbed wire fence, or puking up a demon's brew of refried beans and Cuervo in an alley outside a Tijuana strip joint.

Laura chopped her Binge Dresses off just below the crotch and wore them with black fishnets and garters. While she might not quite have been Hard As Nails, she was *definitely* Cheap As Dirt! Iris and I were really excited to meet someone who was as slutty as we were and who could also keep up with our gargantuan drug and booze intake. The fact that Laura played like a hellion didn't hurt either: she was like a young female version of Keith Richards and Slash

84

from Guns & Roses put together. After a couple of lost weekends together, I promptly drafted her for The Screamin' Sirens. It was just a matter of time until she moved into Disgraceland. One of our mutual boyfriends built a king-sized loft bed for her, and she gleefully moved all   her guitar amps and bass cabinets into the space beneath the bed, which was easily tall enough for her in all her   show girl-sized glory, to putter around wearing her favorite black patent Jackie O stiletto heels.

As Laura became a full-fledged member of my band, she learned the Screamin' Sirens secret language, which had been developed over the course of years in rehearsals and cramped van rides. These unique catch phrases were a verbal punctuation for incidences of drunken mayhem, and always used with gusto, usually in tandem with raising (and spilling) a Burgie beer aloft in a toast.

One of our affirmations was a loud, slobbering tribute to Sylvester The Cat, "YESSSSTHUR", the other was gleefully yelling "SCARED", while making a wide-eyed, mock- frightened face.   As band members and roommates, the overlapping of our sexual conquests had become even more out of control than it was when we first met, so   that Laura and I had taken to exclaiming "*SHARED*" instead of "SCARED". As the Sirens began to tour, the *Shared* joke reached new heights.

"Kick me out *now!*" Laura would yell, as we both went after the same guy, who was   always   the type we'd affectionately started referring to as Big Slobs.

As our touring progressed, Laura and I eventually began to have separate boyfriends. Our favorite squeezes were both members of Poison 13, an infamous Austin - based   sludge rock band. The other Sirens were also hooked up with Texans- members of The Reverend Horton Heat, The Big Boys, and The Hickoids, because we played in Austin, Houston, Dallas and San Antonio quite frequently. On tour, just outside the Texas State Line, all of us would automatically change into our most fetching Binge Dresses and carefully apply our Wet ' N' Wild lipstick as the van sped towards the city that every member of the Sirens had taken to referring as *Ahhhh-Ahhhh-Ahhh-Ahhhh- Austin.*

But while the other Sirens were learning new riffs and maybe getting in a little lovin' in on the side, Laura and I were with our Poison 13 paramours, partaking in The Austin Diet Plan.

The "AD" went something like this: our boys, both of whom had live-in girlfriends, would ditch their chicks and meet the Sirens' van with cases of Rolling Rock beer. On the lame pretense of *getting guitar strings*, Laura and I would be kidnapped by the guys to drunk-drive around Austin, listening over and over to a looped live cassette of People's Temple preacher Jim Jones urging his followers to drink the Kool-Aid, while we did endless rails of Meth... and finally having desperate, clandestine Speed Sex in The Sirens van.

Laura and I were so cranked out that one time as we walked through the door of Austin's Continental Club when Poison 13 was playing, and even though the stage was a few hundred feet away at the back of the long room, we could see the band's bass player Chris Gates' teeth all Speed Grinding to the beat.

We always got secret AD to-go *care packages* from our boys, which meant that Laura and I were pretty much up for the rest of the tour. Even though the rest of the band definitely did as many drugs as we did, the other girls were unaware of the AD, and merely thought Laura and I were dedicated troupers for constantly offering to take the dreaded post-gig all-night drives to the next town. Laura always drove, I was the Co-Pilot (or, in Siren's lingo, the *Cow Pie*) whose duty it was to hand Laura lit cigarettes, speed bumps, Smarties and slurps of disgusting, watery road coffee...not like we *needed* the caffeine.

We saw some crazy shit on those drives. Once in Oklahoma, as dawn was breaking, I saw a Longhorn Steer, lying on it's back by the side of the road. Stiff as a board, all four legs were pointing up to the sky, and it was a completely charred, a cow-shaped cinder block that was still *smoking*. My mind was racing from the Meth, and I thought I might be hallucinating. Finally, after about two miles or so, Laura, her eyes glued to the road, said through her tightly clenched jaw,

" Uh...did you *see* that thing?"

"Yeah...", was about all I could manage. We looked at each other for a second.

"Should we turn back?" I asked.

"Nah..."

Wordlessly, I held up a keyful of The Austin Diet Plan to her nostril. It was proof enough of the steer's existence that we'd both seen it.

Another time, in Maryland, on a twelve-hour drive from Cape Cod to North Carolina, we were stuck in a three-hour traffic jam while the rest of the band slept. There was a huge carnival wreck scattered across all the lanes on both sides of the highway. In the mist and rain, we saw an over-turned semi, with gaily painted Tilt-A-Whirl buckets and glittery, kiddy-ride rocket ships scattered haphazardly across the road. There were two tigers and a lion bellowing from large cages laying wheels-up in the grass on the median, about seven wrecked cars; some ruined Airstream trailers, and an upended snack truck leaking a mountain of popcorn. Laura and I tried to wake up the rest of the band to see this surreal sight, but none of them seemed to think it was as big a deal as we did, and they didn't budge.

While we were touring, we sent many postcards back to Iris, holding the Disgraceland fort down, to let her know what we were up to. Mostly, they were glossaries of the new Sirens slang that had developed on the road, so she'd understand what we were saying and be able converse with us when we got back from our tour.

All that speed was making us horny, and though the other Sirens had a dude in every town, Laura and I had hit a major dry spell... Or maybe it was just that mid-western guys were *frightened* of two meth-addled nympho chicks, dressed in our summer touring outfits, which were...rather *unique*. Laura and I both had multi-colored rags tied into our dreadlocks pickaninny style, and wore way too much make-up along with our artfully ripped, midriff Thrasher shirts and men's boxer-shorts, which we had adorned with studded belts. We rocked fishnets and vintage cowboy boots that were held together with duct tape and festooned with Mardi gras beads and Christmas tinsel garlands, so that we looked like sparkly Clydesdales. "Scared" indeed... *no wonder we didn't get laid!*

By the time we returned to Austin, our home-wrecking shenanigans had been discovered by the mates of our Poison 13 guys, so Laura and I were shit outta luck, both for getting some sex as well as scoring more speed. Pissed off and determined to finish what was left of the AD, Laura and I drove the van home from in one final, speed-fueled long haul through the desert heat. We had an important gig that night at The Club Lingerie with Tex & The Horseheads and the legendary Screamin' Jay Hawkins, and we wanted to try to pull into LA before noon and get some sleep before sound check. Happy to be back at Disgraceland after being up for over thirty-six hours, we were greeted by a twisted scene that shocked even us.

Before we even got out of the van, we heard the theme from "Psycho" playing over and over at full volume on our stereo. The familiar amps and records and empty beer bottles were scattered all over the floor, but something seemed amiss...Iris was nowhere to be found. Three guys that lived At Disgraceland on and off- Stevo of The Vandals, Mike Martt of Tex & The Horseheads and artist Clam Lynch- were there, but though ambulatory, they were in varying stages of severe incoherence. They were also wearing every piece of leopard clothing or accessories-that Iris and I owned-...and we owned *a lot*.

Stevo and Clam stood in front of the stereo, performing a slow-motion ballet that apparently was supposed to be mock Kung Fu fight. Each of them were wearing a leopard opera-length glove on one hand, and had squeezed into Fifties leopard cocktail sheaths worn unzipped over their t-shirts and jeans. Stevo also had on an open leopard clutch on his head, worn like a Fez. They were screaming faux Asian nonsense in crazed falsetto voices, waving steak knives at each other.

Mike Martt, whose mouth was smeared in thick red lipstick like a clown, was passed out cold on the couch, snoring. He was in my leopard-print '60's half-slip and Iris' real leopard fur cape, his feet with their big army sox still on were squeezed into my vintage leopard Frederick's Of Hollywood stiletto heeled mules. On his head was a jaunty 1940's leopard beret and he had a fast food container covering his face like a sleep mask, a giant tomato slice draped over one eye like a melting Salvador Dali Alarm Clock.

The phone rang and Clam answered it, screaming pretend Chinese into the receiver.

Looking at me pie-eyed, he managed to slur,

"Plez, it's your *mom!*"

Already speechless at this scene, my amazement turned to horror. I begged Clam in frantic whispers and Spontaneous Charades to tell her I wasn't here, hoping against hope that he would *comprehend*.

Man, all I needed at this point was my mom knowing I was home, and wanting to come to my gig with all of us in this condition! *How the hell was I going to pull this one off?*

My mother is a very persistent woman. She had also long since resigned herself to the chaos I lived in, not that she liked or approved of it. I guessed correctly that she'd call right back. As if on cue, the phone rang, and apparently she asked to speak to "somebody sober", because, changing rapidly from his Kung Fu alter ego, Clam growled in his thick, hoarse Boston accent,

"THERE'S NOBODY SOBER HERE!"

He tried to hang the phone up, dropping the receiver on the floor in the process.

Realizing it would only be a matter of time til the guys passed out- or, shudder to think- *that my mom came over*, Laura and I retired into my bedroom to try to sleep off the speed. Fidgety and restless, we lay on top of the covers in our boxer shorts and bras. We were both sweaty and covered in road grime, our hearts pumping fast, our eyes tightly screwed shut, and given the circumstances, we were unable to relax. We tossed and turned through "Waiting For Cindy" by the Nip Drivers, "State Of Shock" by Michael Jackson, and then another half hour or so of the "Psycho" theme. Suddenly, it was eerily quiet.

"I can't fucking sleep," I said, forlornly, breaking the silence.

" I can't either," Laura moaned.

The next thing I knew, she was asking me if I'd ever owned a vibrator.

"No," I said, "But I'm not sure why... have *you* ever owned one?"

"Nope".

With that, we looked at each other determinedly, as if we were on a pre-destined mission, guided by *fate*. As though we were zombies with twin brains, we automatically rose from the bed and pulled our cowboy boots on. It didn't need to be mentioned out loud that we were going to the porn store on the corner of Caheunga and Hollywood to get ourselves vibrators...*we both already knew.*

Laura went into the living room to get her things together, and I hesitantly pulled open my closet, eying a threadbare Greta Garbo-esque trench coat as I slapped on my Ray Bans.

"We're gonna dress like perverts in trench coats and sunglasses, right?', I yelled in the direction of the living room, hoping it sounded funny.

"Of course!" Laura said matter-of-factly, suddenly standing in my doorway, wearing a stained olive drab Army –issue trench coat of Stevo's, the belt tied jauntily at her waist, her sunglasses already on and a cigarette hanging from her mouth like a War Correspondent.

We didn't say a word as we walked in step in swift clipped strides down Selma Avenue. As we turned up Cahuenga, I mentioned that I certainly wasn't about to go through with the plan if all they had were giant black rubber dildoes.

"*Oh, god no,*" Laura agreed, cool and business-like,

"We'll just get the standard... like...cream colored *personal massager* type."

I breathed a sigh of relief as we walked through a thick rubber curtain and into the store.

Laura addressed the fat, balding hippy with the gray ponytail behind the counter in her best "lady" voice:

"Um, yes... we'd like to see your selection of vibrators".

The guy motioned to a shelf in a glass case, and there they were, a small line of the standard, putty-beige ones, not an over-sized *lifelike* black dildo in sight. In unison, Laura and I both uttered small but audible gasps as we realized they were only $3.99... they were actually *affordable*- we had feared they'd be far more expensive!

We looked at each other and simultaneously and with conviction said, "*Iris!*"

It was abundantly clear that if both of us had never owned a vibrator, it was a safe bet that Iris never had, either!

"We'll take three," Laura told the clerk decisively, " And can you please give us some extra batteries?"

With our packages secure in their plain brown paper bags, we high-tailed it back to Disgraceland, eager to try out our new toys.

Amazingly, the leopard brigade was nowhere to be seen... It was as though they'd vanished into thin air. But Iris still wasn't home, either, so we left her discreetly wrapped present and the new batteries in front of the door to her room, with a little note that said: FROM YOUR SECRET ADMIRER, and hurried back to our rooms to test-drive our new acquisitions.

I didn't need to draw the shades in my room because there weren't any- the windows were covered in tin foil. I lay back on my sweaty sheets, hiked my boxers over to one side, and turned the vibrator on. I was kind of taken aback that it was so loud, but seconds later I heard a higher-pitched buzzing coming from Laura's loft bed. Our vibrators were making a crazy kind of Appalachian harmony, but I'd barely processed that thought when I began to feel a familiar tingle, a sensation that usually took about twenty minutes to reach. I inhaled sharply, waiting to peak, and just as I did, I heard the other vibrator stop, as well as Laura happily yelling *"No Fucking Way!"* from the living room.

I lay in my bed, spent, and then just as I was ready to try again, I heard Laura's vibrator switch on. This went on all afternoon. It was with great difficulty we tore ourselves away from our new found fun to get ready for sound check and our gig.

Not that it was *unusual* or anything, but our show was a mess. Mike showed up still shit-faced, still in his lipstick and still wearing the leopard cape, which Screamin' Jay Hawkins, who was higher than a kite on what he called Rock Star Weed, was sincerely admiring. The entire staff of Enigma Records, the label who had been foolhardy enough to sign Tex and The Horseheads *and* The Screamin' Sirens, were in attendance, and CEO Ron Goudie had made the mistake of providing a trashcan full of beer on ice in the dressing room, as well as buying us rounds of celebratory drinks.

After we played a black out set, Laura cornered me and whispered conspiratorially that she couldn't wait to get home to *them*, which I instinctively knew was our vibrators.

Screamin' Jay Hawkins signed my Screamin' Sirens "gang" colors that night, and also wound up at Disgraceland- along with half the audience- to smoke more Rockstar Weed, so getting down with our new found addiction was out of the question. Speaking in code, I nudged Laura and said out of the side of my mouth,

"I wish all these assholes would leave so we could play with...*them!*"

She winked at me over our delicious secret. We were so in love with *Them* that suddenly, all the boys we both lusted for had faded away.... they were simply too much trouble!

Hungover and trashed the next morning, Laura and I again engaged in our newfound passion. In fact, not a day went by that week when we didn't.

"Wow, wouldn't it be amazing if we took *Them* on tour?" Laura asked all misty-eyed and glowing one day, as though she was in the first honeymoon months of a new relationship.

"I don't know how we'd do it, " I answered sadly, thinking of the times when at least seven of us slept in the van, parked in a lot behind some dive we were playing.

A bit later in the week, Laura asked me how Iris liked Them, and we realized she hadn't said a word to either one of us. I ran to her door, and noticed with chagrin that the gift we'd left her was still sitting on the table, unopened. A few days later, it was still there. It wasn't unlike Iris- or any of us- to disappear for days on end, but we were anxious to find out if she loved her present as much as *we* did.

More time went by and I actually had to change the batteries on my vibrator.... and then suddenly, Iris slipped back into Disgraceland as though she hadn't been missing for ten days. For some reason, I forgot to ask her about Them, and it wasn't til a week later, at The Frolic Room, that she, Laura and I were all together again.

Over the din of the jukebox, we asked Iris if she was enjoying her present.

"Present? What present?" she shrieked,

"I never got a present from you guys!"

When we explained what it was, and told her how we'd decided to give them to her, a strange expression crossed her face.

"That was from *you guys*?"

We nodded happily.

"Oh, thank *God*," she said, "I thought it was a horrible practical joke from an ex-boyfriend, like an insult or something!"

"Did you throw it away?" we asked in horror.

As she shook her head no, we told her how divine *they* were and that she simply had to try it.

The next morning Iris emerged from her bedroom with a sloppy grin on her face. She plopped onto the couch, slitted her eyes and purred,

"That was... I mean, *Them* was.... *No Fucking Way!*"

CHICKS AND WHIPS:

TALES FROM THE VELVET HAMMER BURLESQUE

All my life I've had a fantasy about being a magician's assistant and getting sawed in half, but prior to my career in burlesque, I never even came close to imagining that I'd be an assistant in a precision bullwhip act; two *different whip acts* in fact, for over a decade.

I met whip-master Brian Chic in 1996 at the Viper Room; we were both performing for a circus-themed private party. Michelle Carr, Hollywood hipster and founder of The Velvet Hammer Burlesque was doing her famous Jungle Girl striptease, during which she disrobed from a full gorilla suit to Screamin' Jay Hawkins' "I Put A Spell On You". I was belly dancing while balancing scimitars on my head and various other parts of my body.

After my show, I watched the whip act, which was so carnie-cool it absolutely fascinated me. The whip-cracks were far louder than the background music while Brian expertly snatched drinking straws directly out of his female assistant's mouth. She wore a leather corset, had badly done chunky highlights in her utilitarian short haircut, and looked like she was half asleep. During the course of their show I became absolutely certain that I would make a *much* better assistant than the dead-pan lady he had with him... but he looked so mean and scary onstage, I was too intimidated to talk to him! Portly and imposing, he wore a full dress tux, and the whip seemed alive in his hand. He was scowling like he meant business and could be capable of murder. Brian handled the whip as though it was his *lover*... and the girl was merely an accessory. He had the air of an off-duty SS commandant who thoroughly enjoyed his job.

Well, that was a cool thing to see, I thought to myself, *I can now add being part of a whip act to the long list of Ridiculous Things I Will Never Do - like riding in The Goodyear Blimp, being an astronaut or a CIA agent ...sigh...oh well.*

Later in the evening, Brian came up to me, his approach nothing short of gentlemanly and affable. He complimented my dancing and asked politely if I'd ever consider being his assistant. Of course I had the good sense to play it cool and didn't tell him that I was *dying* to!

We started working together that very week, and by the next Velvet Hammer show, we debuted our own whip act, which was unlike any other he'd done- because it actually had a storyline and *real dancing*. I named our duo "Lipstick And Lashes", and we performed together for over a decade in The Velvet Hammer as well as various other shows.

The main premise watoo far from the plot of a silent movie melodrama. He was the mean master and I was the naughty slave girl, taunting and disobeying him. The whip cracks, I discovered, were *always* louder than the blasting music, because as the whip flies through the air it literally breaks the speed of sound. The instant the whip wrapped around parts of my body most of it's force was already gone, so I practiced timing my theatrical flinches and agonized expressions to sync up with the cracks of the whip to make it look like I was in dire pain as he whaled on me relentlessly. Witnessing this, the audience would predictably go insane in two different ways: some covered their eyes or even fled the house; others would be yelling like drunken Romans at a gladiator show, out for blood.

The entire time we worked together, we'd have to rehearse not just for sequence, but also for *safety*. Brian taught me the specific and exacting angles where I needed to put my head for various maneuvers, so that I wouldn't get cut across the face.

With his hand-braided bullwhips, he'd savagely switch my belly dance veils out of my hands, crack my costume off my body, then expertly wrap the whip around my neck and I'd spin out of it. At the end of the act, I'd jump into the air landing on the floor in a full split that would've made James Brown jealous, finishing up by posing with one arm overhead. Brian would crack the whip around my wrist and I'd use the whip to pull myself up. Then, in a feminist twist, I'd lead him off-stage. He always followed me all hangdog and docile-*literally pussy whipped*- so it was abundantly clear to the audience that I was the boss!

Off-stage, Brian, who'd been raised in Kentucky, was very straight-laced, reserved and polite like the Southern Gentleman he truly was. He was always very uncomfortable in the dressing room with all the naked, drunk Velvet Hammer chicks running around and screaming- he would sit for entire shows in the dark wings of the stage or in the hallway, silently.

96

We had a serious falling out at one point, so we stopped working together, and even speaking to each other. *It was like a divorce.* I was sad I'd lost a partner, and very bitter. After a year or two apart, we made up and did many more Velvet Hammer shows and other shows until his untimely death in June 2007.

During the period we were estranged, I missed our teamwork, the exotic danger and seedy carnival glamour of Lipstick And Lashes, but I figured I would just do something else in the show- *and never once dreamed it would be another whip act!*

One day, Michelle Carr informed me that Danyell- formerly Slymenstra Hymen of the band Gwar and mastermind behind the all-female sideshow troupe The Girlie Freakshow- was joining the Velvet Hammer. Naturally, Michelle wanted us to do a whip act. Danyell had learned double bull-whips from a couple who'd done it in Ringling Brothers for thirty-five years... but their act was Wild West style and family oriented, so we both figured we'd have to tart it up a bit.

Right off the bat at our first rehearsal, Danyell told me straight up that she'd had an accident with an assistant on a recent European tour...and that she'd literally whipped the girl's eyeball out! Apparently, it had to be surgically re-attached and Danyell was in the middle of a gigantic lawsuit. But as I observed her technique, she seemed *fine* to me- so I just practiced with her taking the precaution of wearing a pair of huge, round 1960's sunglasses as safety goggles.

I came up with the name for our act and also our stage monikers. In keeping with the Western feel, we became The High Plains Harlots. Danyell, dressed as an 1880's-era saloon girl dress with a bustle and corset, became Madame West, The Dominatrix of Dodge City. I was the wild half-breed squaw, Princess Kissameecoochie. We debuted our act at The Velvet Hammer's 2002 Mayan Theater show and did it to The Shadow's vintage instrumental hit "Apache".

Danyell whipped the feathered train off my glitzy faux-Sioux war bonnet, I held large sheets of newsprint paper in my hands and she shredded them into tiny squares, she whipped balsa wood targets out of my hands and mouth and then whipped my white velvet "buckskin" skirt right off my hips. At the climax of the act, I'd remove my feather headdress and take my top off behind it, as Danyell whipped the bra out of my out-stretched hand. Just before the number ended, we planned some Hot Squaw On Saloon Girl Action: I'd hold I the headdress in front our faces and we'd pretend to kiss behind it.

The same night our act debuted, Tura Satana, burlesque legend and the buxom Karate-kicking, weapon wielding star of the Russ Meyers' legendary cult film *Faster Pussycat, Kill! Kill!* was The Velvet Hammer's guest of honor. All day long at the tech-check and dress rehearsal, everyone in the cast was in total awe of her. She was aloof and kept to herself, though once when we passed in the hallway, she complimented me on my costume and feathered headdress. I shivered in private glee. All the Hammer chicks (including me) wanted to talk to her or at least get her autograph... but none of us wanted to disturb her or be intrusive, stalker-ish or just plain old dorky.

Tura Satana was larger than life, a living goddess. Onstage, she was nothing short of amazing... for the climax to her number she languidly laid on her back on the floor, twirling just one pastie at a time! The entire place was going nuts.

During the first show, our debut High Plains Harlots act *slayed* the audience. That first taste of success combined with the very real danger involved made Danyell and me absolutely giddy with adrenalin. We both got completely into character and became carried away- at the end of the act, we started making out for *real*, in full view of the audience onstage, for an awfully long time. Finally, a stagehand had to literally drag us into the wings. We ran giggling down the steep steps of The Mayan's backstage, holding hands and exploding into the dressing room. The show's make up artist Glenn -a leather queen whose entire body was covered in tattoos of Cher- was *horrified* cause Madame West and I both had huge clown- mouths, the entire bottoms of our faces were smeared with lipstick...*and we had a second show to do!*

At The Velvet Hammer, it was practically *mandatory* to drink in the dressing rooms and everyone always brought lots of champagne. During our rehearsals, Danyell and I had made a strict pact to stay sober- not an easy feat at a Hammer show- because we needed to be spot-on, not just for the routine to run correctly, but because of the potential for serious injury. But since our first show had gone so well, we both threw caution to the wind and mutually decided we'd have just a teensy sip of champers. Yeah, *right!* We wound up getting stupendously drunk for the second show- which was extremely stupid of both of us because of the safety issues! Neither one of us even *remembered* our second performance we were so fucked up- but apparently it was great. Not only that, at the end I still had both eyes intact!

Now that our act was a roaring success, of course we had even *more* to drink. Hours before, I'd been silently hoping that possibly I could maybe get a picture with Tura Satana, but like everyone else, was too shy to ask her. But elated after my successful new act and now totally shit-faced, all my inhibitions went buh-bye.

The next morning, I remembered vaguely that I'd posed for a photo with Tura Satana backstage, and as I lazily turned over in my bed full of body glitter, I was smug and happy I had a memento. Regrettably, I was way too hung over to take my film in that day to get developed.

Later that week, when I finally picked up the film roll, the pictures all seemed like average, fun Velvet Hammer backstage shots- lots of beautiful naked women in high heels and full stage make up with curlers in their hair, standing in a sea of suitcases overflowing with sparkly lingerie, brandishing bottles of alcohol. It was just another night at The Velvet Hammer...until the very end of the film roll. When I saw the last five shots, I literally screamed in the middle of the photo lab.

I still have *no idea* who took the pictures, but imagine my total shock to see images of me in pasties and full half-breed squaw glittery war-paint *touching tongues with Tura Satana*...and that wasn't all...shades of Danyell and me onstage, Tura Satana was literally making out with me in the next shot! In the three pictures after that, my boyfriend Dirty, still in full Emmett Kelly clown make-up from his Hobo-Meets-Baby-Carriage number with Selene Luna, stood between Tura Satana and me, while she held his belt in her hand, staring lasciviously down into his open fly!

In 2005, for the Miss Exotic World Pageant at the Helendale location of The Burlesque Hall Of Fame, Tura Satana stood at her table, signing glossies from *Faster Pussycat* and the covers of her new comic book. The line for her autograph snaked around the entire room, but the second she saw me, she screamed,"*Ba-a-a-a-aby!*" and pulled me onto her lap, where I stayed the entire time she scribbled her signature.

Tura Satana and Brian Chic have both left this world and The Velvet Hammer stopped performing years ago... but I cherish all the crazy, whip-cracking, champagne-washed and somewhat woozy memories of those great times more than almost anything I could ever have imagined. It was like running away with the circus.

Riding in the Goodyear Blimp...becoming a CIA agent or astronaut? Small potatoes, barely a blip on my radar screen.

THE SHOWGIRL DIET

Dedicated to the cast of The Velvet Hammer Burlesque

Noon: Stumble out of bed, wiping last night's glitter from your eyes. Wake up with a pot of insanely strong coffee, liberally infused with Half 'n'Half, Down a pint of bottled water. Shower and drink more coffee.

12:30 PM: With a head full of curlers tied in a chiffon scarf, barefoot and wearing a vintage black slip, cook a *huge* breakfast full of protein: two organic dark-yolk eggs over easy, covered in grated Parmesan, sitting atop a ground chicken burger, small side of spinach, one container of Fage full fat Greek yoghurt. You need a big food base to carry you through your day and night! Drink at least two pints of bottled water.

2:36 PM: Pack costumes, chain smoke cigarettes to alleviate hunger pangs. Drink more water.

3:18 PM: Cave to hunger pangs. Chop up a small Persian cucumber into pennies and consume greedily with two rice-stuffed grape leaves and plenty of hummus on the side. Lick the spoon! Smoke more. You are still hungry but can't eat any more carbs, cause you will look bloated onstage if you do. Guzzle water in lieu of food.

3:31 PM: Get a double espresso con panna (make that *heavy* on the panna!) to take to the venue. The extra whip cream is ok...*you're a dancer, you need the calcium!* Sip it in the car, alternating with slugs of bottled water, icy cold and straight from the freezer.

3:45 PM: Rehearsal hasn't started yet cause *some people* are late.

4:22 PM: Rehearsal is about to begin. Grab a giant handful of raw almonds and walnuts to keep energy up while you dance. The Omega 3's are great for sore joints, and once again, *you can't be eating carbs*. Dream of Macaroni And Cheese while you run your number. More cigarettes, more water.

5:00 PM: Time for make up! As you apply your faux lashes, indulge in the backstage vegetable tray, say *to hell with it* and dip into the room-temperature Ranch Dressing...cause it's too close to the veggies to ignore! Feel guilty for being so weak-willed.

6:49 PM: Tech Check: mix up a Showgirl Cocktail. In a plastic or paper cup (basically whatever's handy) two shots designer vodka, mixed into a glass of water with a packet of Emergen-C With MSM. This is good for your joints, and also helps immensely to take the edge off any pre-show jitters! Stagehands drink Red Bull, but dancers don't: there's too much sugar and carbonation and, like practically everything else on Earth, *it'll make you look bloated onstage!* Argue with the lighting designer about your cues. Chain smoke onstage because the house isn't open yet.

7:15 PM: Doors are open! Obsessively check out the crowd through a slit in the closed curtains, squeal over costumes with the other dancers, and finish applying body glitter. Go into the alley behind the theater with a few other performers and smoke.

8:00 PM: Showtime! As the first act begins, the performers start trotting out the bottles of booze hidden in their dance bags. Mid-range champagne is always a good choice, because it goes down smoothly, and since everyone shares, it'd be *foolish* to buy anything expensive! Drink from plastic cups with a straw so you don't wreck your lipstick. The sound of champagne corks popping almost drowns out the strains of the opening number.

8:46 PM: Since everyone backstage is now just a *little bit* tipsy, the "No Smoking" ban in the dressing room has been magically lifted!

9:13 PM: Draft an embarrassed (but extremely happy) stagehand to take some impromptu scandalous photos of all the dancers who are backstage. *Sapphic* is the operative word.

11:00 PM: Miraculously, the show finished on schedule! Down a pint of water, and it's time for The Post Show Mingle With The Audience... graciously allow them to fawn over you and buy you cocktails.

11:50PM: The suitcase that was so diligently organized when you arrived at the theater now will hardly close. Cram still-damp lingerie, one high heel, make up bags, sewing kits, boas, corsets, stray lipstick, curling irons, a flask and any random costume or cosmetic articles you find on the floor into your bag haphazardly.

11:58 PM: Rush to the craft service table backstage along with the entire cast and eat anything that is left over *straight from the package,* including but not limited to: cookies, corn chips, dried out doughnuts, soggy sandwich wraps, potato chips... even industrial-sized containers of coleslaw and potato salad that have been sitting out for hours. Don't worry about the condition of the food; the flasks of Personal Stash alcohol being passed around will kill any germs. Continue to smoke as you stuff food into your face- *but be careful not to smear your lipstick!*

1:00 AM: Frantically look for a parking space near The After Party.

1:13AM: Drag all your costumes and props inside The After Party because you are paranoid about leaving them in the car, in case they get stolen.

1:48 AM: There's plenty of food here, a nice spread, actually... but nobody cares- because there is also *plenty of booze and plenty of blow.* It's almost like Thanksgiving, but with controlled substances!

3:30 AM: Wonder vaguely if you should leave The After Party before the sun rises, but don't move cause someone has once again put out fat rails. Begin chain smoking in earnest.

3:52 AM: Drink almost an entire liter of water before spilling a martini into your cleavage. More rails, more smoking. Eavesdrop on five conversations while simultaneously telling stories of your own.

4:19 AM: Even though you don't smoke pot, take a healthy hit off the joint that's just been handed to you. You don't want to appear rude...and it's not like it's going to *matter* at this point!

4:39 AM: The blow seems to be all gone, so you prudently decide to leave The After Party, congratulating yourself because it turns out you will not be needing the sunglasses you thoughtfully slipped into your purse before you left the house! Consume half a pack of Sugarless Gum to alleviate hunger pangs- *they're baaaack!*

4:56 AM: Look for a drive through... any drive through will do!

5:17 AM: Eat in your car with no thoughts whatsoever of preserving your make up. Notice that the other cars surrounding you are all full of drag queens and hookers also scarfing food with no regard for their make up. Finish the pack of sugarless gum while smoking.

6:12 AM: Your make up, eye leashes, body glitter and pasties are off, your contact lenses are out, your teeth are flossed and brushed and you are slathered in night cream. Wonder what happened to your other shoe while you chase 800 milligrams of Ibuprophen with a pint of bottled water. Cross your fingers that the scary drive through food won't make you look bloated onstage tomorrow.

6:14 AM set the alarm on your phone for noon.

REPEAT.

STALK LIKE AN EGYPTIAN

We weren't expecting to get another kitty.

My boyfriend James and I were still completely inconsolable over the disappearance of Blondie, a beautiful tabby "teenager" who had vanished a few months before.

I was on tour in the UK, teaching and performing belly dance when I heard the awful news, and was totally heartbroken for many reasons. I absolutely adored Blondie- she was a loving cuddle-puss who had been born on my bed to Sphinxie, a young, feral tabby tuxedo whom we had recently managed to tame.

Coincidentally, Blondie's birth had taken place when I was on tour in the UK the year before. That fact alone made her disappearance seem so utterly horrible and surreal that I could hardly comprehend it... there was just something eerie –and terribly finite- about the fact that I was in the same country with the same sponsor when the two most significant events in Blondie's short life occurred.

Every time James called to give me an update-and none of them were good- the pain in his voice broke my heart. Though he loved all our cats, Blondie was his favorite- he had delivered her when Sphinxie was giving birth, and since day one, he and Blondie had been bonded as if by super-glue. She was his little baby, he doted on her shamelessly. A big gruff-looking man, he would sing her lullabies as she fell asleep nestled under his arm in a little tent he had created from the bedclothes.

Apparently, what had happened was: Blondie had woken up in the middle of the night, and somehow knocked over my *shamadan*, a large Egyptian crown with a candelabra mounted on top, which had been stored presumably out of the way on a high shelf. The noise and clattering spooked her, and she ran outside.... *never to be seen again.* A day later, James chased a huge coyote out of our fenced yard, something that had never happened before, but it was an ominous sign.

In England, I felt totally powerless over the situation and I was so sad, overcome with grief and guilt. I felt I was at fault because I wasn't there to help look for Blondie or put up signs in the neighborhood, and because it was *my* candelabra that had set off the chain of events. I also felt shame because I sometimes even wished that this had happened to one of our other cats, grimly thinking that I would have be able to handle it better- James was so disconsolate that I was seriously afraid he would fall into a depression and might never recover. I'd be in the middle of teaching a workshop in London, or in between sets at a show in Leeds, and have to run into the bathroom to weep for a few seconds, before wiping away my tears, stepping outside and acting "normal".

Months after Blondie had gone missing, we were still checking all the Los Angeles shelters for her- *just in case.* We would see a blurry pound picture online and then drive thirty miles to the facility just to be certain that it *wasn't* Blondie.

So there we were, on a warm October afternoon at one of the worst and most over crowded animal shelters in Los Angeles. James and I had to walk by the Feline Pediatric Room to get to the part of the building where they posted the pages with photos of newly inducted animals.The nursery was maybe one of the most wrenching things I'd ever seen, and I had seen plenty of sad things in shelters. The cages took up the entire room, stacked from the floor almost to the ceiling; they were full of young cats- pairs of identical, scruffy adolescent siblings that looked like book-ends, proud queens with full litters of nursing babies, and small, terrified single kittens who'd crammed themselves into the corners of their enclosures, trying to disappear. As we tried not to take in this hopeless sight, we heard a crazy, high- pitched, urgent howling.

Directly at our eye level, in a bare metal cage, was a tiny little striped kitten, all by herself. Her face pressed against the bars as she stuck her arms out of the cage extended straight out, claws unsheathed as she grabbed at the air wildly. For some reason, her cage door was unlocked. My boyfriend reached in and scooped her into his arms, and her howling immediately abated as she snuggled into the space between his neck and shoulder. She began purring immediately, but it sounded asthmatic and congested.

She was dirty and very sick, with matted fur. Her ears were full of fleas, and one side of her nose was almost completely taken up by a jagged, open sore that was oozing pus, an injury that had obviously come from smashing her face into the cage bars in an attempt to free herself. Her eye were crusty and running and there was dried, yellow mucous caked around her nostrils.

106

We put the miniscule kitten back into her cage, and we could hear her wailing all the way down the hallway as we adjourned to the parking lot to have a serious conference about whether we could take her on. Our other cats ranged in age from two and a half to seventeen years; one was a diabetic and another was starting to grow senile. Our cat food and vet bills were staggering and we were both still traumatized about Blondie. Plus, this kitten seemed gravely ill, and in our small house there was no place to guarantee her safe quarantine if whatever she had was contagious.

James then dropped a bomb: he told me he had seen the kitten the previous week, when I was away on yet another weekend at a dance festival. He'd debated internally about adopting her then, but hadn't mentioned it to me because she was ill. But, he added, she had not appeared nearly as seriously sick as she was now. *She was dying.* Amidst us both crying and arguing the pros and cons, we decided to take her.

We went up to the shelter's front desk, waited in a long line, and gave the woman behind the counter the kitten's cage number, saying we wanted to adopt her. It took forever for the worker to look up the paper work, but finally she came back, and with the lackadaisical, contemptuous delivery that only a government worker can muster, she said,

"You can't adopt her. She's only three weeks old, and they have to be eight weeks old and spayed."

Resolute in our decision, I waved the cash for the adoption fee and answered happily,

"Oh, that's ok, we'll just pay for her now and get her when she's old enough!"

The woman looked at me condescendingly and stated,

"We don't *do* that... Besides, that whole room is being put down tomorrow, they're all sick."

Horrified at what I was hearing- *the entire room was going to be exterminated-* I cried,

"But she doesn't have to die! We're pet owners- we *want* her! We'll give her a good home, love and take care of her! We'll give her medicine, and when she's better, we'll get her spayed when she's old enough!"

The woman put her hands on her hips and rolled her eyes before turning her back as a way of wordlessly dismissing me.

I was unable to comprehend the notion that the shelter would let a baby cat die rather than bend the rules a bit and hope that things might turn out well if they took a gamble by letting someone adopt a small, sick, "underage" kitten.

"Is there a vet here?" I inquired politely, "Can I please see the vet?"

The woman went about her business, wholly ignoring me. Beginning to get infuriated with the situation, I started yelling, repeating like an obnoxious parrot,

"I WANT TO SEE THE VET! PLEASE LET ME SEE THE VET...I NEED TO TALK TO THE VET... *LET ME SEE THE VET!*"

After about three minutes of my loud, rhythmic and repetitive chanting, the woman glared at me as though she'd like nothing better than to stab me. She picked up the phone, and covering it with her hand, hissed something into the receiver.

A lot of time went by, and we were beginning to think that perhaps a veterinarian wasn't even on the premises.

After a while, I heard a thickly accented man's voice asking,

"Yes, Madame, may I help you?"

If this was the vet, I thought, *I'd better act quickly and show that I am a very responsible human being...* but before I could think of exactly what I was going to say, I realized that something sounded awfully *familiar* about the inflection in this guys' voice, and for a second, I couldn't place what it was...it just seemed as though I had heard this voice many times before. Looking up slowly, the first thing I saw was nice shoes-doctor shoes- and a lab coat...it was, indeed the vet. He was holding a sheaf of papers in his hand, hopefully the kitten's records. The next thing I focused on was his piercing hazel eyes. He repeated his question, and then it hit me- suddenly I knew why the doctor's voice sounded so familiar!

Without even thinking, I blurted out,

"Are you Egyptian?"

Obviously a little taken aback by this question, the vet answered,

"Yes, I am Egyptian!" He regarded me curiously before asking,

"Why? How you know I am Egyptian- are *you* Egyptian?"

"No," I answered, sure now that my prayers for this little cat would be answered,

"But I go to Egypt all the time!" As an afterthought, I added in Arabic, " *Ana ra'khassah- raks sharqi!*"

When he heard that I was a belly dancer, his eyebrows flew up in surprise. Admittedly, I certainly didn't *look* like a belly dancer... I was wearing sweatpants, my hair was in a sloppy bun, I had my glasses on and it was pretty obvious I'd been crying. *I looked like shit!* I fumbled in my purse for a business card, handed it to him, and he regarded it in disbelief.

"This is *you*?" he questioned, staring at the card.

"Yes, it's me! I usually look better than this.... hey, do you?"

The moment I mentioned her name, he seemed to melt, a trait that is, after all the years since her death, still common among Egyptians. Om Kalthoum, known as *"Kawkab Al Sharq"* or "The Star Of The East" is just as popular and loved nearly forty years after her death as she was when she was alive.

"Oh, Farhaaaaaana", he said, drawing out the syllables of my name luxuriously,

"I looooove Om Kalthoum," he declared passionately.

This lead to a ten-minute discussion about Abdel Halim Hafez, Farid Al Atrache, the Egyptian belly dancers Dina and Lucy, composer Mohamed Abdel Wahab, and our favorite current Arabic pop songs. Finally, I couldn't stand the suspense any longer, not that I wasn't enjoying our conversation. Leaning in close to the vet's ear, I whispered,

"So, listen, I really *really* want this cat..."

He glanced over her papers, smiled conspiratorially, and announced in a sly whisper,

"No problem- she is eight weeks old!"

As James, who had been left out of the conversation entirely, stared in amazement, the vet began scribbling down some completely preposterous, implausible excuse as to why the cat wasn't actually three weeks old, and also noted that she was too sick to have gotten spayed.

"She looks like an Egyptian cat", I pointed out.

"Yes, she looks one hundred percent Egyptian!" the vet declared, commanding us to wait where we were for a few moments.

Presently, he returned with the kitten, a certificate for a free spay, and a week's worth of antibiotics in pre-measured droppers. We signed the papers, and suddenly, we had a new kitten. As she rode home in a makeshift cat carrier-*ok, it was a shoebox from my trunk*– we decided to ask our elderly neighbor if the kitten could stay at her house until her respiratory infection cleared, so our other cats wouldn't catch it.

As I looked over the baby's paperwork, I discovered she had been named Bella at the shelter. I was absolutely positive she'd been given that name by one of the sullen teenage volunteers they had there- kids who were working off their juvenile offenses by doing community service. It was pretty clear that some *Twilight*-obsessed sixteen-year-old gang chick had named the kitten Bella, after Kristen Stewart's role in the vampire film. I was about to suggest we change the kitten's name, until I thought of one of my favorite belly dance costume designers, Bella of Istanbul.

That night, James stayed in our elderly neighbor' guest room, with the baby on his chest, wheezing and sneezing until it got light out. He said that at one point, he'd been afraid she wouldn't make it, but she had- and she grew stronger every day.

A week later, as little Bella tore around the bed pouncing on things that weren't there, my phone rang. It was the vet, asking how Bella was doing. When I told him she had stopped sneezing, gained some weight and was looking fluffy and alert, and that her nose was healing up well, he sighed,

"Hamdalillah!" which means "Thank God" in Arabic.

110

That was a long time ago.

Bella turned into a sleek adult, long, elegant and lean. She still had the giant ears she did as a kitten, and when she sits a certain way, she really *does* look like an Egyptian statue. Her nose has a small scar from her wound, but she is gorgeous, with glossy fur covered in crazy, circular tabby whorls. She and Sphinxie are best friends, and the other cats love her too. She is the light of our lives...and strangely enough, she also shares many of Blondie's unique personality traits, including sleeping up on the shelf near my *shamadan*, which makes James and I wonder if somehow, all of this was meant to be.

* In an unbelievably tragic twist of fate- again parallel with Blondie-, Bella disappeared on August 31, 2012. Because she was such a social kitty, we hope she was picked up by a well-meaning stranger... if not... rest in peace, our little beauty.

HARVEY REDUX

Are you The Easter Bunny?

The question was screamed at me top volume from about thirty feet away as I sat at an outdoor café on LA's trendy Vermont Avenue, sipping a latte. The person inquiring was of indeterminate sex and laboriously pushing a creaking, rusty, overloaded shopping cart. The enquirer had dead leaves scattered through it's hair and also suffered a cleft palate or some similar speech impediment, so it took me a few pointed hollers to realize that the query was, in fact, if I was The Easter Bunny.

Phonetically, the question sounded like this:

"AAAH NYEW NEE EADOR BAAAAHNNEE?"

In my *Flashdance* style cut-off sweatshirt and fresh-from-dance-class sweats, hair piled on top of my head in a sloppy bun and men's aviator shades, I really didn't look anything like The Easter Bunny, or the other patrons of the café... who were beginning to stare at me, wondering what my answer was going to be. It was perfectly clear to everyone within earshot that this question was being hollered directly to *me.*

I'm not sure exactly what it is about me that invites attention from the mentally unstable, but whatever it is, I've got it in spades. Luridly made-up bag ladies routinely cross busy streets just to strike up a conversation with me; blackout drunks at Mardi Gras stagger blindly through police lines to gift me with beads, and I've been the subject of plenty of unsolicited amorous attention from colorful individuals whom law enforcement officers would probably classify as The Criminally Insane. In the two most memorable cases, this, for some reason, has something to do with Easter.

The question was screamed at me again, this time with an urgent note of utter desperation.

Are you The Easter Bunny?

Having now attracted the attention of passers-by as well as all of the other café patrons, I figured I might as well answer.

"Um, no... I'm sorry, I'm not The Easter Bunny,"

I said sheepishly, regretting having inadvertently disturbed everyone's tranquil spring afternoon. Somehow, this didn't daunt my inquisitor. The person continued,

"But do you have an Easter Bunny costume?"

It was now clearly too late *not* to engage in this bizarre exchange, since the whole block seemed to be waiting breathlessly for me answer. Grandstanding for a moment, I yelled back,

"Well, as a matter of fact, I *do*!"

"With bunny ears?"

"Uh, yes, of course with ears!" I replied, wondering just what the hell this was leading up to.

Because of my affirmative answer, the person broke into a manic, jubilant grin revealing many missing teeth and yelled,

"YOU MEET HE HERE ON EASTER MORNING- AND BRING A BASKET WITH CHOCLATE EGGS!"

"Okay," I managed weakly, hoping that it wouldn't shatter the dream when I didn't show up as promised.

Not too long after that, I was walking along Hollywood Boulevard minding my own business, when something similar occurred.

"Hey Pretty Lady, Pretty Lady! Hey can I ask you a question, Pretty Lady?"

Again, I was out in public, looking like- for lack of a better description- ten pounds of shit in a five-pound sack. I blithely ignored the smooth *playah* cadence of this pick-up artist's voice and kept walking quickly hoping to ditch him, but to no avail. Pretty soon, the dude got into step right beside me. Even though my eyes were focused straight ahead, I could tell he was tall and slowing his pace to match mine.

"Hey Pretty Lady! Are you single, do you have a boyfriend? Are you married? You sooo pretty, Pretty Lady!"

114

This went on for at least a block. *Persistent motherfucker*, I thought to myself. *Hopefully he'll see some slutty tourist with a fake tan and a tube top and forget about me.* Out of the corner of my eye, I caught glimpse of his leg as he strode alongside me. He was wearing trousers with a satin stripe down the sides and black jazz oxfords...but they were totally filthy and worn out.

"Hey Pretty Lady! Wanna have some coffee with me, Pretty Lady?"

He wasn't relenting so, as with the previous situation, I figured I should just stop and confront him.

"Pretty Lady! Let's have some coffee and talk about *our future*, Pretty Lady!"

I halted dead in my tracks and before turning to look at him I yelled,

"I'm married!"

"Oh, Pretty *Laaaaady*," he sighed dejectedly.

He was indeed tall. Like, Los Angeles Lakers tall. He was a striking African American man wearing a tuxedo...but the suit was so completely rumpled and covered with caked-on mud, it looked like he'd been run over by a tractor. He also had on a pair of brand new white plush bunny ears with pink satin lining, and he was sporting a child's white plastic *Phantom of The Opera* mask!

For an moment, I considered taking a cell-phone picture with him and maybe even going out to coffee to see what, exactly, his get-up was all about, but then I got a hold of myself, mainly because he smelled so horrible.

Before skipping away from him as quickly as possible, I yelled as loudly as I could manage,

"Are you The Easter Bunny?"

THE FIFTH DATE

When I tell people I've had maybe four dates in my entire life, they think I'm kidding. *Yeah, sure, you're from Hollywood* they say, like I'm always turning down invitations to premieres, wrap parties and après Oscar soirees from Brad Pitt and George Clooney.

Oh, I've had plenty of relationships- not to mention numerous affairs, love triangles, on-going fuck buddy assignations and one-night stands... as well as trysts, booty-calls, and hook-ups. But it's the honest truth: punk rock ruined me for dating. The way I was socially conditioned, you went out for the night -or out on tour- and when you wound up with someone and had sex, the next day you both knew it was either a little fling or the beginning of a relationship. Dinner and a movie? Wining, dining and flowers? I had no clue. This was not *my* reality.

A few years ago, after a lengthy and traumatic break-up, I figured it was about time to get my ass back in the arena, and hell, maybe even *date*. Conveniently forgetting my Junior High level of dating inexperience, I prepared to jump into the fray and be a social butterfly, dating different people every night.

I met Enrique at Go-Go's rhythm guitarist Jane Wiedlin's Weimar Republic-themed birthday party. The music was cranked, champagne was flowing, and there were two strippers in 1920's drag writhing around on the coffee table. To add to the Berlin Between The Wars feeling, guests were attired in leather trench coats, flapper dresses, even Eric Von Stroheim-style riding britches. A male servant with a bleached crew cut, copious amounts of eye make up and a Hitler Youth uniform was chopping up cocaine on an antique stand from a church that had once been used for holding Holy Water.

Grabbing a flute of Cristal, I stepped over the leashed slaves huddling on the floor to get a better look at a guy who definitely stuck out in the crowd. He was, for lack of a better word, a "hunk". Tall, bronzed and body-builder-buff, he had a curly, oiled pompadour and teeth that were so white they couldn't have been real. He was wearing *slacks*, a fishnet body shirt, and a big gold medallion. It was as though Erik Estrada- by way of Chippendale's- had been dropped into the set of *The Night Porter*.

"Isn't that guy hot?" I whispered to a drag queen standing next to me, who was also captivated,

" Do you think that's a costume, or is he for real?"

Tossing back errant strands of hair from his Louise Brooks wig, the queen's immediate response was:

" *Giiiirl*, if he's straight, you should *totally* fuck him!"

Might as well expand my horizons, I thought. *DATING!*

Out on the terrace, a coterie of my gay male pals were ensconced around a table, deep into speculation about the mystery hunk.

"Oooh miss thang...all that's missing is a mullet," cooed one.

"Or a pony-tail!" sighed another.

"He's the *suitcase pimp*," said my friend Willy, daintily sipping a champagne cocktail.

"Huh?" I asked, baffled.

"He came with the strippers."

As if on cue, the scent of very pungent men's cologne filled the air as a prelude to Enrique's entrance, which immediately hushed everyone on the patio as they all went into observation mode. He made a beeline to me and introduced himself in a heavily-accented voice dripping honey. When he said "Enrique", his R's rolled like no tomorrow, like an announcer on a Spanish Top Forty radio station.

I asked what he did; he answered that he was an actor.

"Well, of *course* you are," I said, my tipsy flirtatiousness barely concealing my utter sarcasm. Why else would he look that way?

He turned out to be funny, smart and charming, in town from Venezuela to work on a TV show. It was-*as if it wasn't perfectly obvious*- a soap opera. I later verified with a *telenovela*-addicted girlfriend that he was actually a big daytime TV star in South America, but at this point, I didn't care. It was all kind of funny and exotic.

As I left the terrace to visit the powder room, Enrique followed me up the stairs, his eyes glued to my buttocks, commenting in his silky Fernando Llamas voice,

"Nice view!"

It took him three weeks to call me, but when he did, he apologized, saying he'd been on vacation " in Cabo", *a perfect place,* I thought, *for a guy who wore fishnet body-shirts and probably spent his free time downing Jell-O shots with strippers who were Pamela Anderson look-alikes.* Thankfully, I resisted the urge to ask if he'd seen Sammy Hagar there… mainly because when he called, I was literally out on a limb.

A stray cat had brought three kittens into my house, and on their first venture outside, one had gotten stuck up a tree. I tried to ignore it; it would figure out how to climb down by itself with it's own natural instincts. Stressed out and cranky, I was already late for a photo-session. It was smoggy, about 103 degrees and humid… my false eyelashes weren't sticking, and I was about to get my period at any second. But the kitty was so tiny and so scared; I woke up my actress/model/bartender neighbor and forced her to hold a rickety ladder while I climbed up into the tree to rescue the panicked baby. I was covered in sticks and twigs, sweating profusely. My neighbor broke an acrylic nail and was whining about it…and her hangover. The kitten was wailing, and I was beginning to think maybe I should call the fire department. The walk-around landline phone was shoved into my back pocket; I'd been trying to call the photo studio to say I would be late. When it rang, I answered, assuming it was the photographer.

Enrique laughed when I told him I was up a tree, thinking I was kidding.

"Joo are an interesting girl," he said, intimately, as though he knew me. *You don't know the half of it*, I thought.We made a date for that night.

The photo session sucked. Not only did I feel bloated and ugly, the "studio" was in a garage behind the Fatburger on Santa Monica and Gardner. There was no air-conditioning and the smell of grilled onions permeated the air. I got my period, and also got a flat tire on the way home. By twilight, the heat hadn't let up. But Enrique called again to cajole me into going out, and I figured a cocktail would do me good. He picked me up in a new car that smelled like one, with a metal flake paint job that gleamed as seriously as his teeth.

"*Joo look maaaaah-velous*," he purred sincerely, and I reveled in his ultra-clichéd Don Juan/ Suavecito/Rico Suave cheesiness.

I selected a bar called Daddy's on Vine Street, because it was nearby and dark ...but more importantly, *air-conditioned*. My sisters and I had recently discovered it, having gone there once to toast the memory of our deceased Papa on Father's Day. I remembered it as being quiet, but when we got there, it was absolutely packed with what seemed like the entire cast of every season of *American Idol* contestants. Enrique and I stood at the bar, unable to talk because of the din, and had martinis while waiting for a booth to open up. Finally, one did- it was cozy and intimate. Enrique immediately ordered another round. I felt light-headed, and remembered that due to the kitten, photos and flat tire, I had forgotten to eat. I tried to switch my position, but my platform boot got wedged in the cramped space between the couch and coffee table, so I swung my legs up onto his lap, effectively breaking the ice.

"So," he asked, stroking my legs with one hand and practically bottle-feeding me my martini with the other,

"How did joo lose your virginity?"

Just as I was about to answer, a woman's voice screamed into my ear:

"EXCUSE ME!! CAN WE SHARE THIS BOOTH WITH YOU?"

I turned around and it registered how pretty the girl was. Then, in a dreamlike spit-second, I realized it was my sister Eddie... and that it was so dark, she also didn't recognize *me*. A second later, we both shrieked loudly in shock. Even over the noise of the crowd, our screaming duet was so loud it caused Enrique to spill the martini all over both of us.

"THIS IS MY SISTER," I yelled.

"WHAT IS SHE DOING *HERE*?", Enrique yelled back.

"IT'S JUST A COINCIDENCE!", I screamed back in disbelief, laughing hysterically. *What are the chances?*

Enrique looked dubious, and then I noticed that my sister had in tow her twin Cupcake, both of their boyfriends, and another pal to boot.

"CAN WE SHARE YOUR BOOTH?" Eddie howled.

Flustered but ever the gentleman, Enrique moved over,

"JOO ALWAYS BRING YOUR SISTERS ON DATES?" he bellowed.

"YOU'RE ON A... *DATE*?!?" The twins managed to raise the decibel level to new heights in shocked unison.

The whole crew all crammed into the booth, and ordered us two more rounds, one for intruding, and one just because. Since conversation was nearly impossible and their scrutiny was so intense, Enrique suggested we go back to his place.

"I have vodka there," he hollered.

When we got outside, stumbling into the still-stifling night air, I realized I was beyond tipsy. I was drunk as a skunk. The ride to Enrique's apartment was a blur, although I *do* recall the hellish scent of his aftershave filling the car, and that I couldn't figure out the seat belt and he had to do it up for me.

As we pulled into his driveway, I imagined what his apartment looked like- I just *knew* it would be a bachelor-pad. Not the sloppy, plaid couch and leftover pizza-box Monday Night Football kinda place, but a swinger-ish, sterile *playah* kind of place. I clairvoyantly saw Ikea-type brushed metal CD stands filled with lame R&B, an eighties black lacquer bedroom set, and triptych Southwestern paintings. Maybe a copy of Playboy or a car magazine laying on the glass coffee table. A gooseneck lamp, track lighting on low. *What could I possibly have in common with this person?*

I was immediately thrown into a moral dilemma:

Would I...could I...fuck a guy who had Eighties furniture?

I should have recognized this as a portent of disaster, but decided instead to continue with my anthropological experiment. The interior was worse than I thought. He switched on the stereo, and some god-awful New Age crap was playing. I took a seat on a big, plush cheap couch upholstered with Jackson Pollack / Art Director Scrawl splashed material, while Enrique made drinks. He handed me one, immediately getting out a bong and offering me a hit.

I cannot smoke reefer. I just can't handle it at all. I turn into such a raving lunatic, that it's impossible for me to even form the simple sentence,"I'm so high" without collapsing into painful hysterical laughter complete with tears, aching sides, and snot shooting from both nostrils. I used to joke that I'd only ever smoke marijuana if I were on three or four other substances.

So I politely declined the offer, we sipped our drinks, and made small talk. He got really high quickly, giggling like a school kid, his deep dimples looking adorable. He was giddy and fun, dropping the Latin Lothario thing. *Cool,* I thought, *a new side of this guy, all little boy*! Still woozy from the booze, I remembered I had a tiny bit of coke in my Santee Alley Luis Vuitton knock-off wallet. He refused, saying he didn't do it, but I figured if *he* was indulging in something I didn't do, then it wouldn't be rude to snort it by myself. It energized me and woke me up, but instead of snapping me back into reality, it merely enhanced my drunkenness.

Maybe I wanted some pot after all. Enrique made it look so... attractive. I took a big, bubbly hit, and as it filled my lungs, I immediately got incredibly, ridiculously high.

"It's good stuff, huh?" he choked, holding in another hit.

"Can you turn this shit *off*?" I asked abruptly, gesturing towards the stereo in a dismissive sweep.

He seemed kind of hurt, but obliged.

Change the subject, I thought, *deflect your bad-manners faux pas.*

"Say your name." I commanded, rather loudly.

"Joo know my name," he said looking at me quizzically.

"But just say it, so I can *hear* you," I whined.

"ENRRRRRRRRRIQUE" he said, and I yelped loudly, bouncing up and down in delight. He started snickering at my display.

"SAY IT AGAIN!!!" I yelled. This was turning out to be *fun*.

He repeated, "ENRRRRRRRRRQUE!" and this time it was so gratifying I couldn't contain an orgasmic squeal, getting so excited I knocked my drink all over the carpet.

"Shhhh!" he said, making a gesture to Quiet Down while trying to mop up the mess.

As he went to make another drink, he took a large geode off a shelf and handed it to me.

"Look at that," he called from the kitchen, "Isn't it incredible?"

It was *beyond* incredible… huge, oddly shaped, almost like a stone boat. It was so heavy I had to hold it with both my hands, like a big meteoric watermelon slice. The outer shell was rough, bubbled, pockmarked and rust-colored like iron ore, but the inside was filled with thousands of otherworldly aquamarine crystals, clustered together in all shapes and sizes. Some were milky, some iridescent. It seemed to glow from within. I was rendered speechless with its beauty.

"When I found it on the beach in Cabo", he said, stirring the drinks,

"Only about two inches were sticking up from the sand! Can you believe it?"

I held it up to the light to admire it, turning it slowly, but it seemed to emanate it's own light. Suddenly, holding it and observing it just wasn't enough. I had an overwhelming urge to *taste* it. If it looked this way, certainly it must taste … like…some luxurious outer space wintergreen candy…or at the very least, salty and wonderful like the tropical waters of Mexico.

Ok, the 80's furniture was one thing-I could stretch my personal boundaries to accept that. But I instinctively knew that, stoned or not, there'd be no way in hell Enrique would understand my desire to lick his crystals. *The need to taste it was irresistible.* I stole a furtive glance at the kitchen, and thought maybe I could sneak in just one satisfying taste on the sly. He'd never be the wiser! Swiftly I brought the rock up to my mouth, but sadly, due to the marijuana, I had lost most of my motor control skills. As I lifted the geode to my lips, I misjudged the distance and the boulder smashed me in the face. I was so shocked that I dropped it, causing the entire apartment to shake.

Jumping at the noise, Enrique spilled both drinks, and ran to my side. The whole bottom of my face was numb. I could taste blood filling my mouth, and sliding my tongue tentatively around my front teeth, my heart sank as I felt a jagged edge.

I babbled what I hoped sounded like, "Did I chip my tooth?"

Enrique gently took my chin in his hand, trying to discern the damage done to my face.

"Well," he said slowly, " Maybe just a *little*,"

Full of adrenalin, I raced to the bathroom to get a look in the mirror, and tripped over his gym-bag, sailing through the air like Superman before falling flat with my full body weight hitting floor in a sprawled–out heap, this time shaking not just the apartment, but probably the entire building. Picking myself up with great difficulty, I staggered to the mirror and when I saw the chip on my right front tooth, I began to cry inconsolably.

Enrique offered ice in a Whole Foods bag as I blubbered. When the swelling went down and the blood stopped gushing, I demanded to go outside. By now it was about four am, and Enrique was not at all enthused by the idea. Outraged that he didn't think I had enough party-savvy to behave for the neighbor's sake, I had completely forgotten the fact that I'd not only been screaming hysterically minutes earlier but also had dropped the huge rock and then fallen down myself.

Reluctantly taking my arm Enrique brought me onto the terrace for air. It felt good, it felt healing. *I needed oxygen!* He practically had to drag me back in a few minutes later.

Pouting, I flopped onto the couch and crossed my arms like an irate five-year-old in the throws of a tantrum.

"I need *air!*" I whined obstinately.

"Please...", he pleaded, "We have to be quiet!"

By begging non-stop I finally wore him down enough to open the door a sliver. Then I took a drastic measure, a last resort, since he was being so *mean* ...and I needed air.

I lay down on the floor with my nose to the crack of the door, like a dog. Finally relieved, I opened my eyes and noticed he was staring at me. In what could only be described as a colossal understatement, I mumbled,

"I should go…"

"No!" he said swiftly, "Don't go!"

Even in my deteriorated condition, this struck me as straight outta left field. The only reason he could *possibly* want me to stay, I realized, was for sex. But who in their right mind would have a fling with a drunken, stoned, gakked-out, swollen-faced maniac who was laying across the door sill, gasping for air? Who would want to make out with a meteorite-licking wackjob who not only had reefer-induced cottonmouth, but bloody lips and a chipped tooth? *What a sicko!* More than a little concerned at this turn of events, I said I'd call a cab.

"I'll drive you," he offered, to which I replied without an ounce of social convention,

"NO WAY!

He'd been smoking much more of the pot than I had, and if I was in this condition from just a couple of bong hits, how in God's name did he think he could operate an automobile?

Enrique handed me the phone, but I was too wasted to even dial the number for Celebrity Cab, which I'd committed to memory two decades ago. After three attempts, he grabbed the phone and, rolling his eyes, dialed it himself.

I don't remember most of the ride home, but *do* recall the cabbie asking me if it was ok if he picked up a hooker. Bouncing her head and entire spine against the front seat and plexiglass panel, cackling incoherently and way too high on crack, she almost gave me hope that maybe I *wasn't* the most fucked up person on earth. As a gesture of good will, the cabbie didn't charge me for the ride.

I woke up the next morning on my couch, fully clothed, with dry contact lenses adhered to my corneas, and my false eyelashes still intact. That afternoon, while carefully repairing my tooth, my dentist asked me how I'd managed to chip it.

"I... bit into something," I said. It sounded reasonable.

Two weeks later, Enrique left a message on my voice-mail, asking me to go out again.

I never called him back.

DANCERS FEET

Dancers feet are scary.

If you haven't seen them up close, you wouldn't know this...like most of the general public, you're completely deluded. *You* probably think of a ballerina pirouetting in gleaming pale pink satin pointe shoes, or maybe a ballroom dancer gliding around the stage in strappy metallic heels. Possibly you see a Rockette in fishnets and pristine character shoes, a sassy burlesque gal strutting around in darling vintage baby doll pumps, a street dancer in brand new unlaced Chuck Taylors or a barefoot belly dancer with a perfect pedicure, a mehndi design fetchingly winding up her arch?

Get real! As we dancers all know, that's way off mark.

Dancers feet routinely take a beating, and it *shows.* The feet of any professional dancer or avid dance student-no matter what age or experience level, are full of blisters, thick calluses, split skin, corns and bunions. If the dancer works barefoot as many styles of dance require, then you can also add "filthy" onto the list, because even when a barefoot dancer scrubs and pumices her feet, they still appear grimy and soiled because of all the calluses and ingrained dirt.

The plain truth is, most dancers have feet that are undeniably frightening- in fact; they give most zombie movies a run for their money!

I have dancers feet- oh, you bet I do.

Before I started belly dancing, I went barefoot habitually so I already had the calluses and dirty-looking thing goin' on, but as much as I liked feeling the grass or beach sand underfoot, I was never too fond of my feet. They served their purpose well, but they were never what anyone would call *aesthetically pleasing.*

My feet are small and square, almost as wide as they were long. I have the feet of my ancestors: tough little dogs that had apparently been designed for standing hours on end in a soggy Ukrainian field, harvesting a meager crop of potatoes. I used to joke that the appearance of my feet was akin to the way the bottom of The Coward Lion's costume in "The Wizard Of Oz": boxy and grubby.

When I first began to dance, I felt even felt a bit of *foot-shame*. Like most civilians, and many dance novices, I thought that dancers were supposed to have dainty, high-arched feet that matched the preternatural beauty of their bodies in motion...and mine just didn't match up to the fantasy.

Boy, was I wrong... and I heaved a sigh of relief, feeling as though I had just joined a wonderful secret society, a club where everyone's feet looked like they'd been through a war. I no longer had to make excuses for my battered, banged up tootsies- I now had an excuse, *I was a dancer*! My messy-looking feet had finally brought me home.

When I started performing, I made every effort possible to have my feet look presentable...so I could preserve the glamorous illusion for the sake of my audience. I'd sleep with my feet slathered in Vaseline, encased in a pair of thick socks. I obsessively carried nail polish in my gig bag so I could touch up my ghetto-looking toes before hitting the stage.

I got frequent pedicures at my Korean-run nail salon, but it was kind of pointless. It was like when you see a car driving around with a totally smashed in bumper that the driver has tried to repair with duct tape...making the damage seem even more visible. I always felt a little nervous going to my nail salon, like I was some kind of an imposter trying to pass an identity test, because most of the other patrons weren't dancers and they all seemed to have perfectly groomed, impossibly soft and pampered feet.

Finally, at the salon, I found Anna, a nice Korean lady who did great work repairing my feet and making them seem almost *human*. Though her English was toddler-level at best, Anna was always cheerful as she'd scour away the layers of dead skin. Plus, she gave great massages that went all the way up to the knees. I tried explaining to her that I was a dancer, but I don't think she ever comprehended what I was saying.... she'd just smile and nod. But Anna intuitively understood which calluses needed to stay and which needed to be destroyed. She'd bend over the wreckage that was each foot, working diligently and keeping up a constant, happy murmuring chatter in Korean with the other technicians.

Once in a while, Anna would wave the nail polish I'd selected and look me directly in the eye, beaming at me and whispering,

"Ni' color ... *men like!*"

I always tipped her sumptuously, and truly believed we had a *rapport.*

Because I didn't want to offend her in any way, I'd taken to trying to do a bit of damage control before each appointment, trying to make my scary feet presentable. Pre-professional pedicure, I'd be neurotically soaking, scrubbing and pumicing my feet at home, trying valiantly to get them up to the level of the sorority girls or stay-at-home-mom's feet that I felt Anna was used to dealing with.

One day, I had a pedicure appointment directly after a class I was teaching. Since I wasn't at home and couldn't do my usual pre-pedi cleansing ritual, I reached into my dance bag to grab a baby-wipe, and at least get rid of some of the surface grime. To my horror, the package was empty.

By this time I was already in the car, and also running a bit behind. I wasn't late yet, but I would be if I went back into the studio to rinse off, or to stop and purchase more baby wipes. Blithely, I made the decision to show up with my feet as-is for my appointment... after all, I was Anna's regular customer, we *knew* each other...she'd understand!

As I hurried into the salon, Anna was already set up at her station, waiting for me.

"Hi Prince'!" She said in her low, polite voice,

"You *late*... you forge' appoin'men' with Anna?"

Contritely, I explained that I had just come from class; I kicked off my flip-flops and stuck my feet in the tub. To my shame, the water immediately turned a muddy dark gray. There were actual specks of studio-floor dirt and debris floating on the surface. Feeling guilty, I had an urgent need to address the situation and apologize for it, so I confided my predicament to Anna in a conspiratorial tone.

"I'm sooo sorry," I began,

"I just came from dance class, and my feet are... uh...well, they're kind of *dirty*."

Anna abruptly cut me off, her voice rising to a decibel I'd never, ever heard her reach previously.

"OOOOOOOOOOH, PRINCE' ! ", She bellowed in an accusatory tone so loudly that every manicurist and patron in the salon whipped around to stare at me in disgust,

"YOU FEET ALWAY TERRIBLE!"

A SIGN FROM THE UNIVERSE

I don't normally get stage fright, but admittedly, I was quite nervous to be performing at The 2009 Ahlan Wa Sahlan Festival. Let me amend that statement- I wasn't just nervous, I wanted to throw up. I kind of had a sick and hollow feeling in the pit of my stomach from the moment I'd arrived in Egypt, just even from *thinking* about it... and of course I couldn't *stop* thinking about it!

It was my first year as an instructor at the festival in Cairo, one of the largest belly dance events in the entire world. This fact alone was kind of hard for me to believe, considering that many of the other instructors were people I had been idolizing since the very beginning of my dance career. Their artistry and fame were absolutely legendary. Just some of the Egyptian dancers who were teaching and performing were Mona El Said, Dina, Aida Nour and celebrated choreographer Raqia Hassan, the festival director.

If you compared the world of belly dance to the realm of rock 'n' roll, this would mean that I was about to perform with Elvis, Roy Orbison, Jimi Hendrix, The Sex Pistols and The Beatles. Every one of these Egyptian artists had been wildly famous for decades... *and they were all going to be in the audience that night!* So yeah, I felt like I was about to go full-blown into a panic attack!

Even with my increasing dread and heart palpitations, I'd had the classic Egyptian song *We Deret El Ayam* going through my head for at least the past week and a half. Made famous by the illustrious Om Kalthoum, the song is heartbreakingly beautiful- not to mention one of my all-time favorite Arabic songs. Now was my chance to perform to this gorgeous piece of music, played by a live band in the city where it was created. Steeling my shot-to-hell-and-back nerves, I told myself that I shouldn't be a coward or a quitter; I would do this, I *could* do this. Yes, in fact, I *needed* to do this, even if I felt like an imposter in front of the celebrated dancers I'd adored for years, even if I was so ruined with jetlag that I was no longer sure I would *ever* sleep again, even if failed miserably. I'd dreamed about this for years- now it was happening- and I was considering *not doing it?* I pushed myself well past my comfort zone and proceeded ahead.

The light at the end of the tunnel appeared when I found out that The Henkesh Brothers were going to be playing for the dancers that night, and like most belly dancers on the planet, I was familiar with their work. The leader of the band was Khamis Henkesh, an incredible drummer who came from a Cairo family who'd been musicians for generations. In his lifetime, Khamis and his talented relatives had all played for some of the most famous belly dancers from Egypt as well as from other countries. They'd also made many recordings, which are treasured and regularly used by performers all over the world. A festival representative instructed me to find Khamis Henkesh so we could discuss the music for my set, and I crossed my fingers that no one had selected *We Deret Al Ayam* so it could be *mine*. If I was going to do this, it might as well be to my favorite song!

After running around the halls and the massive belly dance *souk* at the Mena House Hotel for a good forty-five minutes, I finally located Khamis on the mezzanine. He was sitting in a corner of a corridor on a folding chair, drinking Arabic coffee and smoking, his *tabla* resting on his lap. After a brief introduction, Khamis and I began to "discuss" my music.

"For you, Farhana, I will play *Enta Omri!*" he announced decisively.

Now, I love the wistful *Enta Omri*, it's a striking Om Kalthoum classic. The only problem was, I was going completely OCD on *We Deret El Ayam*. Plus, I'm a bossy American chick who, impending panic attack or not, wasn't going to let a drummer *who didn't even know me* –no matter how famous he was- tell me what he was going to play for me without at least a *little* dialogue about my musical preference for my performance.

 I was kind of hoping to dance to *We Deret Al Ayam*," I said in my best honey-silk girly-girl Egyptian back-up singer voice.

"No, I think *Enta Omri* will be better," Khamis said, taking a long drag of his cigarette.

"Oh, but I really *really* want to dance to *We Deret Al Ayam!* " I said, batting my eyelashes.

132

"For you, I play *Enta Omri!*" Khamis declared,

" You will one hundred percent like this music!"

"Is someone else dancing to *We Deret Al Ayam?*" I inquired, valiantly hoping I was still sounding flirtatious.

After a long, contemplative sip of coffee, he said no.

"You know *We Deret Al Ayam*, right?" I asked, as desperation began to seep in. I needed to dance to it, dammit!

" Of *course* I know how to play this, " he said in exasperation, "But I think for you, *Enta Omri* is better!"

Because he was so emphatic and I was so jet lagged, it would've pr been a done deal at that point, my performing to *Enta Omri*... except for the fact that at that *very second*, man in a suit approached us as he walked the hallway. Just as the man passed by us, his mobile phone rang...and the insanely loud Arabic music ringtone that blared from his phone was *We Deret Al Ayam*!

Khamis and I both stared in dumb amazement as the stranger passed by us. An incredulous expression passed over Khamis' face for a moment before he threw up his hands in a gesture of surrender. His eyes widened and darted around before he looked directly into *my* eyes and said sincerely,

"Farhana, for *you*, of course now I play *We Deret Al Ayam*..."

 With that, he shook his head, and we both watched silently as the stranger with the phone disappeared down the hotel corridor.

Then Khamis said,

"*Aiwa*...yes... I *must* play this song for you, together we will make beautiful show!"

And we did.

Internationally famous Egyptian drummer Khamis Henkesh passed away in the late summer of 2012...May he rest in peace.

LADY DON'T BE PANIC!

The fat businessman flashing his brassiere in the middle of the street should've been a red flag, but being a Hollywood native, stuff like that happens to me on an everyday basis, so it took a moment to register that I wasn't at home, but in Cairo. I'm a freak-magnet. Weird circumstances and insane people actively seek me out. Once in a while, the way five-year-old girls dream about being Katy Perry or Selena Gomez, I have fantasies about living like "everybody else"- but no matter how hard I try to behave, to act *normal*, it never seems to work.

It was 1999, and I traveling with my friend Tracy. We both belly danced professionally, and had been to Egypt before, but this time we were in Cairo for the first ever *Ahlan Wa Sahlan* Dance Festival, featuring classes and workshops by legendary choreographers of *le danse orientale*, many of whom had been famous for decades. Performers from all over the world were attending. We'd been giddily planning this trip for months, leaving messages blasting Arabic pop on each other's answering machines, saving every penny for dance classes and costumes.

We were not only excited about going to Cairo, but more than happy to leave our everyday lives behind. Tracy was going through a nasty divorce; I'd been dealing with veterinary and automotive problems on a constant, nightmare level. Counting the minutes 'til our departure, we breezily waved away everyone's concerns over terrorism. *Anything would be better than what we'd both recently been through!*

Tracy's mom, a nice Jewish housewife from the San Fernando Valley, was almost as excited as we were. She stuffed Tracy's suitcase with munchies, trial-sized shampoos and travel accoutrements, and even scored us a bottle of Valium for the plane. But the *piece de resistance* was the tiny, state-of-the-art video camera she gave her daughter so the entire trip could be documented.

"This is gonna be so great!" Tracy gloated, standing in the middle of LAX, stroking the camera in a gesture not unlike a lover's caress,

"We're gonna be able to record every little thing that happens to us!"

The second we stepped off the plane, conservatively dressed, trying desperately to look and act like average tourists, the Fellini shit started. It began with the hotel, which was a dump, even by Third World standards. We'd both agreed to staying in a budget place, being tough chicks who'd back-packed through Europe, camped out on beaches and deserts and stranger's floors. We didn't *need* cushy surroundings, we both reasoned, we'd hardly ever be there!

The lobby of Hotel Amon Toushka said it all. There were a couple of dead palm trees sitting in decomposing clay pots filled with cigar butts and crumpled up tissues. Old men loitered smoking *sheesha* pipes, their ratty turbans and food-stained *galibiyyas* barely visible through the haze of stale smoke. The desk clerk was a nastier-looking, vampirical version of Sirhan Sirhan. We considered offering him a pen-for some reason, Western style pens are in huge demand in Egypt, and are considered a status symbol that can also be given as tips or tokens of esteem- but it didn't seem as though it would change his sneering attitude. He demanded our passports immediately, as though he'd sell them on the black market the second we stepped into the elevator. Fortunately, it took almost fifteen minutes to come.

The creaking ride up to our seventh floor room was terrifying; we expected to plunge to the lobby with every lurching second. We wended our way down a narrow corridor, barely lit by naked light bulbs. The dirty salmon-colored walls were punched in every few feet; threadbare oriental carpets littered with piles of chipped plaster and discarded food wrappers were spread haphazardly over bare concrete.

We weren't surprise to see that our room wasn't made up. Damp, ragged towels covered the floor, and sagging beds revealed dirty sheets interwoven with black pubic hairs. The sun-bleached curtains had once been a gay Flower Power Seventies print, but were now torn and rotten, falling off their hooks. The indoor-outdoor carpeting was stained with grease and a dead radio hung by its own wires from a trashed cabinet within the bedside table. Amazed to see a television set, Tracy tried to turn it on and the front control panel fell off.

There are only two phrases one needs to know to survive in Cairo. One is *In Sh'Allah*, which means "If God is willing" in Arabic; the other is No Problem. They are used ubiquitously as well as inter-changeably, covering everything from the answer to a simple question to the rationalization and/or solution for a major emergency. If something is going to happen, it will...*In Sh'Allah*, so you wait—*No Problem*—as long as you need to, until Allah decides the outcome.

Delirious from lack of sleep and urgently needing to flee the flea-bag after hearing forty five minutes of "*In Sh'Allah*" and No Problem from the front desk (without tangible results) regarding everything from getting clean linens to making an overseas call, Tracy and I locked our valuables in our suitcases and made for the street. We waited the requisite half-hour for the elevator. Looking for the stairs, I opened an emergency exit door and made the rather unsettling discovery that the hotel simply *did not exist* between our floor and the lobby. There were four steps and then six stories of twisted metal and raw cement-courtesy of the last earthquake- with no stairs or even floors between the ground floor and us!

Walking down one of Cairo's main thoroughfares, Giza Street, between the Ministry Of Culture and the upscale Cairo Sheraton, we were approached by a tubby, balding man in Western clothes. Seemingly reaching for his cell-phone, the guy lighting-quick unbuttoned his shirt, revealing a dingy JC Penney's-style, no-nonsense, grandma-type brassiere. It was so threadbare and dirty it couldn't even *begin* to qualify as lingerie- even a bag lady on crack would've been ashamed of it! Looking directly into our eyes as he passed, he tongued his lips lasciviously and squeezed his left nipple. Stunned and speechless, I asked Tracy:

"Did that *really* happen?"

"I can't believe that just happened!" she replied in amazement.

Our first impulse was to reach for our cameras, but by the time we had them in hand, the man was gone-the soldiers guarding the Ministry Of Culture hadn't even noticed him. *But we sure noticed them.* And it wasn't just their snowy white Tourist Police uniforms, a beret tilted jauntily to one side. *How hard is it to miss lithe, café au lait-skinned nineteen-year-olds with Pharonic features and puppy-dog eyes— especially when they're smoking casually, wearing gun-belts and packing gigantic automatic weapons?*

Since our cameras were already out, we tried for a photo-op. Instead, we succeeded in attracting the attention of their first in command, a pot-bellied, toothless guy who screamed in broken English that we were violating an Egyptian law we didn't even know existed: it is illegal to take pictures of anything having to do with the military. As we left, Tracy whispered, "No Problem!" launching us both into fits of punchy giggles.

That night, we were determined to paint the town, even though I'd developed a nasty bladder infection. We'd been guest-listed to see the Dina, the most famous belly dancer in the Arabic world. Dina is a household word, like Madonna or Barbra Streisand. We couldn't believe our good fortune! At 9:30 we began our toilette. By 10:00, we discovered the shower wouldn't turn off. By 10:15, we'd begun a frantic series of calls to the front desk. When 10:30 arrived, the bathtub had begun to fill up, and the whole room was inundated with steam.

"No Problem," said Sirhan Sirhan, in a lackadaisical, offhand tone.

Soon the bathroom floor was completely flooded, so I called again at 10:45, and tried to describe in detail, slowly and clearly, what was happening.

"LADY, DON'T BE PANIC!" he hollered in disgust, banging the phone onto the receiver.

I calculated that we'd need at least twenty minutes for the elevator to come, so if we weren't going to miss Dina, we'd have to leave now.

"Fuck it!" I said to Tracy, "We're *outta* here!"

We piled our suitcases on top of the dressers, left the windows open for the water vapors to escape, and bailed, drenched as though we'd come out of a steam room.

Dina was awesome, with her huge orchestra and multiple costume changes. The highlight of the show was when she danced to "Al Atlal" by Om Kulthoum, and the entire crowd lost it. Om Kulthoum, for those who don't know, is to the Arabic world what Elvis is to Westerners...*and then some*. Like The King, after she died, she became even more famous, as though canonized. Every cabby in Cairo has a picture of her in his wallet. The first time I heard Om Kulthoum, I was an immediate convert. Then I saw her picture...and, well, let's just say that she makes Fat Elvis look dignified. The passion in her voice is stunning, and she was gorgeous in the 1940's, but towards the end of her career, she was old and bloated, and didn't really manage to cover it up in voluminous caftans. Nearly blind, she wore oversized Jackie O sunglasses and she had a number of double chins, which were only *accented* by her massive bouffant hair-do. She always sang with a white handkerchief in one hand—some said it was because her songs were so full of sadness and longing; others insisted it was because she was an addict who concealed cocaine in her hankie, sniffing it onstage during her lengthy concerts. Whatever... the handkerchief, like the glasses and scary hair, were her trademarks. I must say that Om Kulthoum, more than any living human being, resembles those scary old beehive haired ladies in the comic strip "The Far Side." But even mention her name and Egyptians get misty-eyed.... and seeing Dina dance to a thirty piece orchestra playing Om Kulthoum made me and Tracy so crazy we *had* to go out and party with George, a jovial Lebanese guy we'd just met.

We went to the Mena House Oberoi Hotel, right near the Pyramids, where George managed the casino. We all got shitfaced on his tab, listening to stories about the multitudinous times he'd been arrested in various countries; then he took us to an after-hours disco. Somewhere along the line, his name got changed to "G-Dog." Just before the sun came up, we went with G-Dog to his place, right around the corner from our hotel, to have a nightcap of *Arak* (an Arab version of Pernod or Ouzo) with juice and smoke a s*heesha* pipe before turning in.

Tracy and I arrived back at our room after the day had officially started. Unbelievably, the shower wasn't running. Utterly inebriated and jubilant that our entire room wasn't soaked, we documented the hotel room's splendor with Tracy's video camera. We showed off every carpet stain, duct-taped piece of furniture and mildewed towel, reaching new heights of delirium, laughing so hard we ached, and then we discovered that the shower hadn't been fixed—*they'd merely covered up the problem by turning our water off!*

A series of phone calls to the front desk ensued; all met with the standard No Problem. By the time the plumber arrived, accompanied by a shifty-looking, unsettlingly quiet security guard, it was so bright in the room, and Tracy and I were wearing our shades.

"Look, it's the *water doctor!*" Tracy cried, sticking the camcorder in the men's faces the moment they came in through the door.

She giggled drunkenly and filmed everything, from the Arabic curses streaming out of the plumber's mouth as he wallowed on the bathroom floor getting soaked, to my slaphappy, slurred commentary and "Hey, Culligan Man!" jokes. Finally, the water pressure was restored and the guys left.

Brushing my teeth with my sunglasses on, my hair wadded up into a sloppy bun on top of my head, I was struck with my uncanny resemblance to Om Kulthoum. Grabbing a bed-sheet and draping it around my body to fashion a caftan, waving a piece of Kleenex in my hand, I stepped onto the balcony and started prancing around, bellowing phonetic lyrics to the famous Om Kulthoum song, "Ya M' Sharni" at the top of my lungs. Tracy filmed my psychotic histrionics with the Nile as a background, until I stepped inside, laughing so hard the sheet fell off.

"Keep singing!" Tracy cried, maneuvering camera angles like a guerilla filmmaker, "Do X-rated nude Om Kulthoum!"

Of course, I obliged her.

*　　*　　*

We spent most of the next day jet-lagged and seriously hung over, in a cab circling endlessly around Cairo looking for a post office. The one we finally found had a mud yard with chickens pecking around inside the lobby. Exhausted by the nearly one hundred and twenty degree heat, we sat down at a café. We needed caffeine so badly we were practically sobbing. After waiting ages to have our orders taken and longer for the coffee to get made, the waiter dropped the tray with our drinks just as he approached our table. Maintaining our composure, we actually smiled at him as he slowly shuffled his way back to the kitchen.

Finally, my spoiled American need for *instant gratification* surfaced, mixed with my pounding hangover, and I let loose with a full dose of cranky, culture-shocked sarcasm.

"Trace- you know the Six Day War?"

"Yeah...". she grunted, gamely trying to gear up for a political conversation.

"If it takes this long to get a coffee," I sighed,

"I just can't see how it's within the realm of possibility that an *entire* war could've gotten started and finished within a week!"

She grinned at me haphazardly, her bloodshot eyes wandering off in two different directions.

*　　*　　*

It wasn't until late that night, still functioning on zero sleep yet about to go clubbing again, that Tracy noticed her camcorder was missing.

"Are you *sure*?" I asked, thinking it was just buried in her suitcase jumble of blow dryers, workout wear, pantyhose and lunch-box sized snack foods.

"It's gone," she said mournfully,

"I looked *everywhere*."

Our luck was such that Sirhan Sirhan was on duty again, so I went to the lobby to call world-famous choreographer Raqia Hassan, who directed the dance festival, because she spoke fluent English. Meanwhile, Tracy came down to the lobby and started shrieking, causing a major scene. Sirhan Sirhan, the hotel's manager, and all the old men sitting around smoking *sheesha* stormed up to the room, throwing everything around, arguing with each other in Arabic and trying to find the camera, which they figured we crazy, rich Americans had merely misplaced. All they succeeded in doing was, as we call it in the States, Tampering With A Crime Scene. In other words, they destroyed any evidence that might have been left behind and put their fingerprints all over our belongings. Raqia sent over one of the festival's representatives to act as a liason. Mohammed arrived looking like a slick, 1980's-style Vegas gigolo, or maybe a near-Eastern version of Don Johnson in *Miami Vice* dressed head-to-toe in silver sharkskin.

Pissed off and keyed up as she was, Tracy took one look at Mohammed, and began covertly pointing at him, frantically mouthing to me,

"*He's cute!*"

Trying to be serious, even in the face of Tracy's cartoon-like libidinal display (in spite of his garish taste in clothing, Mohammed *was* pretty damn easy on the eyes) I kept a straight face and attempted to answer questions posed in broken English. Tracy alternately ranted, giggled, eyed Mohammed lasciviously, and wept.

"There, there, *Trashy*," Mohammed said, mispronouncing her name as he patted her back, while she gave me a sly sidelong glance,

" *Trashy*, please, don't be hysteric! Is OK... *no problem!*"

Mohammed had me write up a statement for "Trashy" to sign, flashing his silver Bic pen for us to use. At this point, we'd been in Egypt long enough to be duly impressed—a man is only as good as his pen, after all! So this posturing was Mohammed's way of saying he was on top of the situation. He assured us that Egyptian police were *very clever*. Out of sheer nerves, Tracy and I were compulsively munching our way through her stash of junk food as Mohammed stared in disbelief.

Just then, with a dramatic gasp, her hands flying up to her mouth, Tracy remembered that the missing camera contained footage of my nude Om Kulthoum act, something I'd thought of grimly the very moment she discovered the camera was missing. In fact, I was reasonably sure that my nude concert was all over the Internet by now. With renewed fervor, Tracy told   Mohamed it was an absolute necessity she get her camera back, and pulling him aside, urgently stage-whispered that there was footage of me *naked*. At this, Mohammed's eyes nearly popped out of his head in shock over the sinful and incomprehensible antics of Loose Western Women.

"We must get the camera and tape back," he said, gravely.

Then, giddy with testosterone and brightening at his good fortune to be in a room with two women who would commit such a licentious act, he leered at me pointedly and said,

"So I can see this!"

After more Arabic arguments with the contingent from the lobby, who were chain-smoking cigars at a rate equal to our junk food consumption, Mohammed made it clear that it was crucial for us to go to the police station to make a report. As Tracy and I grabbed our sweaters, Mohamed looked us over dubiously.

"Ah...I mean no offense," he said as politely as he could muster,

"But you cannot go to station looking like..." He threw his hands heavenwards,

"Like... one hundred percent... *nightclub womens!*"

Obediently washing off our glitter make-up, we changed into baggy, covered-up modest clothes. Staring into the closet, I noticed my Levi jeans had also been stolen.

Even though it was fucked up that we'd been robbed, and that we weren't going to go out to see Lucy or Fifi Abdou dance, we both were a little excited and adrenaline-charged with the prospect of going to Police Headquarters in Cairo. It would, after all, be An Adventure.

The moment we entered the station our illusions were shattered and we started to get frightened. It was as though we'd stepped out of a James Bond movie and into *Midnight Express*. As our eyes adjusted to the dim, flickering fluorescent lights, we took in the cracked, filthy linoleum floors; the rat traps in the corners; the battered file cabinets, their drawers open and bulging with folders; not to mention the surly-looking, middle-aged cops lounging on dilapidated Naugahyde chairs,

142

nonchalantly cleaning their Kalashnikov machine guns. Tracy gripped my hand so hard her bubble gum-pink acrylic nails dug into my palm. Mohammed and the head cop started yelling at each other immediately.

"*Not Without My Camcorder!*" I whispered, trying to put Tracy at ease with a joke.

Mohammed motioned us frantically to be quiet as the head guy, who had a huge, raised scar down one cheek, stood up abruptly, adjusted his gun-belt in a macho pose, and said to Tracy in deadly calm, perfect English,

"Whom do you wish to accuse?"

"Accuse?" Tracy asked, her voice barely audible and quivering with terror.

"Yes, you must *accuse* someone!" the cop said, his gaze steely, as he took out a long knife and began tapping it impatiently on the desk.

Tracy stood silently, suddenly looking very small and young, her eyes darting around nervously before finally meeting mine. I felt skittish; my breath was quick and shallow as I took in the whole situation, sizing things up. Self-preservation tactics and escape plans began running through my mind. It seemed as though… maybe we should just…forget the whole matter, go back to the hotel, get some rest, take it easy…perhaps do some light sight-seeing the next day…. Chalk up the camcorder as a loss… and say *anything* to get out of this situation. What's a camcorder, anyway? *Just a material possession that can be easily replaced.* And really, what would happen if they did get it back, and- *oh my God!* - saw Naked Om Kulthoum, *then what?*

Quickly, reality hit me along with waves of dread. I felt panicky about what I'd done on film, what I'd done so thoughtlessly in a foreign country. *Was I out of my mind?* To me, at the time, it was just tipsy shenanigans. If I had done this at home in Hollywood, it would've been a *joke,* even with the cops, but what about here? Surely, there were laws about nudity not to mention lewd conduct—*was I completely insane? What the hell was I thinking?* Egypt may not be as hardcore about morality and religion as Saudi Arabia, Afghanistan or Iran, where women are mandated to veil and not even allowed to drive, but still, it's an unbelievably conservative country, with all but about two percent of the citizens made up a devout Muslims who pray five times a day.

I had the distinct feeling that what I did would *never* fall under the umbrella of Allah having willed it, and there'd be *no way* I could never explain away my flagrant display by saying No Problem. Totally horrified, suddenly I felt the need to pee. Badly.

"Mohammed," I whined, like a kindergartner about to have an accident,

"I have to go to the bathroom!"

Tracy was biting her cuticles, saying nothing as Mohammed regarded me and said emphatically,

"But Farhana, you cannot go to the bathroom here. You must wait."

I resigned myself, rationalizing that it was just nerves and not my bladder infection, trying to breathe deeply and think calming thoughts, when the hotel's plumber was brought in, hands cuffed behind his back, looking absolutely terrified.

The cops roughly threw him onto a bench facing us and began harshly interrogating him. I openly stared at his cheap rubber sandals, worn-out pants and his haggard face, and felt horrible. He looked like a nice guy, a decent sort. It didn't seem as though he would steal anything. He probably had a wife and kids at home in a cramped apartment in Ezbet Khairalah.

Soon, my remorse changed to desperation: after another forty-five minutes of everyone in the room screaming at each other, my teeth were floating.

"I have to go to the *bathroom,*" I said urgently, pummeling Mohammed.

"You cannot go to the bathroom!" he hollered,

"THIS IS BATHROOM ONLY FOR CRIMINAL!"

"I have a bladder infection!" I yelled right back, as all the policemen's heads snapped around like Linda Blair's in *The Exorcist.*

"But listen to me, Farhana" Mohammed said carefully, as though he was talking to an obstinate child or someone with a severe mental disability,

" You must wait. This bathroom is...*inhuman!*"

"I'm going to wet my pants," I said truthfully, through gritted teeth.

144

Another agonizing ten minutes went by as Mohammed attempted to explain my situation to the cops, who regarded me suspiciously. Finally granted reluctant permission, Mohammed took my hand tightly, and with an escort of two cops, I limped down a corridor to the toilet.

There were a bunch of men loitering around in pimpy-looking 80's sweat suits with pagers and cheap cell-phones prominently displayed. I noticed that they were   linked together chain-gang-style with Medieval-looking iron leg-shackles.

Standing near them was the most over-the top, freakish hooker I'd ever seen. Even if she'd been a character in a Tarantino or John Waters film, she'd have been hard to believe-she momentarily made me forget my bloated bladder. Tall and corpulent, she wore a luridly patterned mis-matched skirt and low-cut blouse which looked even more psychedelic than it already was under the strobing fluorescent lights; the cheap, sparkly fabric nearly bursting over huge, melon-like, stretch-mark-scarred breasts. Shiny taupe Spandex tights encased her sausage-shaped legs, leading to white pumps almost completely black with scuffmarks. Her massive, badly permed hair was bleached a sickly shade of Creamsicle orange, filled with plastic flowers. Her clown-like make-up resembled Joel Grey's "Emcee" character in *Cabaret*—two symmetrical circular splotches of red on her pock-marked cheeks which complimented the harsh, silvery blue shadow that almost—*but not quite*—hid a huge shiner. She was handcuffed, and on one of her scratched and hirsute arms, wore bangle bracelets up to the elbow. From the noise they made—a tinkle, rather than a clank—it was obvious they were real gold, a fortune's worth.

The guards went into the bathroom first, roughly dragging a man in traditional *Saidi* dress out, as he protested violently. Actually, the toilet was not really any worse than many other Egyptian bathrooms I'd been in…except for the fresh feces smeared on the walls. There were two metal foot-forms on the floor flanking an open hole in which to relieve you. No toilet paper, no light. As I urinated and endless stream, sighing in relief, Mohammed guarded me, providing a human barricade so no one could open the door, which didn't have a lock. I could see his Italian loafer-encased feet planted firmly, inches from my own, outside the stall door.

Back in the main room, Tracy was still sitting morosely, looking small and scared, squirrelly at being left alone in this hellhole. More arguing ensued. Perhaps "Trashy" had brought the camera to Cairo only to lose it *intentionally*, so as to collect insurance? How did we know in fact that the perpetrator wasn't one of the hotel maids?

We valiantly tried to explain that Tracy had never even insured the thing, and if she had, wouldn't it have been much easier to just "lose" the camera in Los Angeles…why go through all the red tape of doing it in a foreign country-one with a *different alphabet*?

We both were positive that the culprit was the suspicious-looking hotel security guard who'd accompanied the plumber. First of all, the door hadn't been forced, so it was obviously an inside job. Second-and more importantly-the security guard was the only person besides the plumber who'd even *seen* the camera. And the plumber was here, shitting bricks, probably thinking he was about to get his hand cut off or something.

Plus, both Tracy and I thought it odd that if indeed the thief had been one of the naïve- looking teenage chambermaids, why hadn't they stolen any of the multitudinous beauty products, costume jewelry or feminine clothing we'd left out? The only item stolen other than the camera was a pair of Levi 501's- the coveted American men's jean that would've fit the security guards *perfectly*. With the severe language barrier, all this was impossible to translate to the police.

Ultimately, Tracy was made to sign a statement that she couldn't even read—it had been typed up in Arabic. We were finally allowed to leave, just as dawn was breaking.

" I feel as though you are my *sisters*," Mohammed said, darting expertly through Cairo's kamikaze traffic, apparently forgetting about being all hot at the possibility of seeing my nude Om Kulthoum karaoke act.

As he dropped us off in front of the Amon Toushka, he handed us his business card, saying he would get the matter sorted out, which we severely doubted. Relieved to be done with the whole incident, we'd both written off the possibility of ever seeing the camcorder again.

We immediately started packing our belongings, planning a hasty exit. There was *no way* we were going to spend even another minute in the hotel. Tracy called G-Dog, who was just arriving home from his casino job.

"Guess where I've been?" she shouted hysterically shrill and almost gleefully into the phone,

"I've been in *jail*!"

After hearing an abbreviated version of our ordeal, he commanded us to get a cab to his house immediately. We could stay with him, he offered chivalrously, or he would help check us into a Five Star hotel. As Tracy struggled with her overstuffed bags, waiting impatiently for the elevator, she suggested taking the stairs, too delirious to realize that all her luggage would've been totally unmanageable.

"Let's just wait," I sighed, too exhausted to explain to her that there was nothing but air between our floor and the lobby.

As we tried to beat a hasty exit, attempting to forego the proper checkout procedure with Sirhan Sirhan (whom we never, *ever* wanted to see again) the scene at the front desk could've been any random newsreel footage of people trying to escape a war-torn country as a coup took place. Everyone sitting around the lobby, all the old men, even a bunch of newly arrived, jet-lagged, hippie-looking Norwegian tourists, got involved. Sirhan Sirhan was going apoplectic, pounding on his ledger, shrieking and gesturing wildly.

On the street, the cabbie we'd just flagged down and bribed with a ten-pound note, was simultaneously stuffing our luggage into the trunk of his car while bellowing loudly, violently engaged in a duffel bag tug-of-war with the Tourist Police, who'd been summoned by Siran Sirhan. We finally escaped, and safely at the entrance to G-Dog's building, I started laughing hysterically while Tracy broke down in the tears that had been threatening all night. At this point, we hadn't slept more than four or five hours in like…six days.

Later that day, we checked into the Ramses Hilton, where the Ahlan Wa Sahlan Festival was being held. The employees at reception were charming and fawned all over us, sending our bags up to our room with a crisply-uniformed bellhop and offering us gratis cocktails that we gulped gratefully while we waiting for the paperwork to go through.

We were amazed at the cleanliness and luxe modern amenities of our room. Feeling like we'd won the lottery, we noted the sparkling clean bathroom with a tub, shower and bidet, and the fluffy, pristine bath-towels, tiny soaps and lotions neatly sealed in Hilton wrappers. There was a big-screen color TV that actually *worked*, double beds, and a phone whose receiver wouldn't give you hepatitis, trench mouth or some leprous skin condition. Putting on our bikinis, we went down to the pool, crashed onto chaise lounges and ordered more liquor immediately, charging the cocktails to our room.

After the dance festival started, Mohammed came by, wearing a Mafioso-like combo of a black polyester shirt and skin-tight, white-brushed denim jeans, which unfortunately showcased his beefy thighs.

147

Shiny-faced and sweaty, he had bags under his eyes, was in need of a shave, and reeked of cheap cologne.

"Still no news on your camera, Trashy," he said, trying to look all in charge and official with his clipboard.

We knew through the belly dance grapevine that he'd been bungling matters all week, including taking care of some other festival attendees staying at the Amon Toushka, who'd also had property stolen from their rooms. As he fumbled, flipping through some papers looking for a police document Tracy needed to show at customs upon departure, Tracy and I both eyed him critically. There were wet rings of perspiration under his arms and his hands were shaking.

Leaning in close to me, Tracy whispered cattily,

"You know, Mohammed's not really that cute... he's kind of a dork... and he's sort of fat."

I nodded in agreement.

"All he really has going for himself," Tracy yawned, the entitled Valley Girl in her coming out,

"Is a *good pen*!"

Mohammed was a harried, stressed-out mess, a Polyester disaster, a buffoon... a mere shell of the capable, take-charge guy he's been just days before. Chunky and inept, he was almost endearing in a pathetic sort of way. He'd put up with a lot- from *us*, especially. Feeling a wave of pity, for a few seconds, I wished he could see my Om Kalthoum impersonation after all. It'd do him some good, cheer him up, and possibly restore his former macho jauntiness.

Tracy and I did our best to appear grateful. We both tried not to roll our eyes as Mohammed continued earnestly,

"...But the police, I am sure they are working on your case..."

"Yeah, *sure* Mohamed," Tracy said, all blasé and sarcastic, cutting

him off mid-sentence while catching my eye. She continued,

"I know -*one hundred percent*...the police, they are *very clever*!"

Her sarcasm sailed with an almost audible swoosh right over Mohammed's head as she drawled, "*No Problem!*

PLEASANT GEHMAN

Pleasant Gehman is a true renaissance woman: writer, dancer, actor, musician and painter. A Hollywood icon, during the 1970's, she was one of the first punks in Los Angeles, documenting the scene she helped create in her fanzine "Lobotomy". During the 1980's, she toured across North America fronting her three bands, all of whom released recordings: The Screaming Sirens, The Ringling Sisters and Honk If Yer Horny. She was also the booker for the seminal Los Angeles clubs Cathay De Grande and Raji's.

Since the early 1990's, under the stage name Princess Farhana, she has appeared internationally and a professional belly dancer and burlesque performer and teacher. She has danced and acted in numerous motion pictures, in music videos and on television. She has appeared in many documentaries on belly dance and burlesque, performing and as an interview subject. In 2009, she was the star of Steve Balderson's film "Underbelly: A Year In The Life Of Princess Farhana" which was released worldwide in theaters as well as on DVD.

From the age of sixteen, Pleasant worked as a journalist and cultural commentator with literally thousands of articles published nationally and internationally on everything from rock 'n'roll to homeless teenagers. Her memoirs, short stories and poetry have been widely anthologized and many works were recorded on her spoken word CD *Ruined*.

She is the author and/or editor of eight books.

www.pleasantgehman.blogspot.com
www.facebook.com/pleasant.gehman
www.facebook.com/princess.farhana
www.twitter.com/PleasantGehman1
www.princessfarhana.com
www.princessraqs.blogspot.com

OTHER BOOKS BY PLEASANT GEHMAN

Senorita Sin

Princess Of Hollywood

Escape From Houdini Mountain

The Underground Guide To Los Angeles, Vol. I, II,III

The Belly Dance Handbook

Other Punk Hostage Press Titles

Fractured (2012) by Danny Baker

Better Than A Gun In A Knife Fight (2012) by A. Razor

Drawn Blood (2012) by A. Razor

The Daughters of Bastards (2012) by Iris Berry

Tomorrow, Yvonne. Poetry & Prose For Suicidal Egotists (2012) by
Yvonne de la Vega

impress (2012) by C.V. Auchterlonie

miracles of the BloG (2012)
by Carolyn Srygley-Moore

8th & Agony (2012) by Rich Ferguson

Beaten Up Beaten Down (2012) by A. Razor

Small Catastrophes in a Big World (2012)
by A. Razor

Moth Wing Tea (2013) by Dennis Cruz

Untamed (2013) by Jack Grisham

Made in the USA
Lexington, KY
25 September 2015